Intimacy Through Hearing

Listening When God Speaks

Paul A. Gilbert

Copyright © 2020 Paul A. Gilbert

All rights reserved

No part of this book may be reproduced, or stored in a retrieval system, or transmitted in any form or by any means, electronic, mechanical, photocopying, recording, or otherwise, without express written permission of the publisher.

ISBN-9798682530489

Library of Congress Control Number: 2018675309
Printed in the United States of America

All Scripture quotations, unless otherwise indicated, are taken from the Holy Bible, New International Version®, NIV®. Copyright ©1973, 1978, 1984, 2011 by Biblica, Inc.™ Used by permission of Zondervan. All rights reserved worldwide, www.zondervan.com The "NIV" and "New International Version" are trademarks registered in the United States Patent and Trademark Office by Biblica, Inc.™

Scripture quotations marked (AMPCE) are taken from the Amplified Bible, Copyright © 1954, 1958, 1962, 1964, 1965, 1987 by The Lockman Foundation. Used by permission.

Scripture quotations marked (NLT) are taken from the Holy Bible, New Living Translation, copyright © 1996, 2004, 2007, 2013, 2015 by Tyndale House Foundation. Used by permission of Tyndale House Publishers, Inc., Carol Stream, Illinois 60188. All rights reserved.

Scripture quotations marked (NKJV) are taken from the New King James Version®. Copyright © 1982 by Thomas Nelson. Used by permission. All rights reserved.

Scripture quotations marked (TPT) are from The Passion Translation®. Copyright © 2017, 2018 by Passion & Fire Ministries, Inc. Used by permission. All rights reserved. ThePassionTranslation.com.

Scripture quotations marked (ESV) are from the ESV® Bible (The Holy Bible, English Standard Version®), copyright © 2001 by Crossway, a publishing ministry of Good News Publishers. Used by permission. All rights reserved.

Scripture taken from the Modern English Version are marked (MEV). Copyright © 2014 by Military Bible Association. Used by permission. All rights reserved.

Scripture quotations marked (CEV) are from the Contemporary English Version Copyright © 1991, 1992, 1995 by American Bible Society. Used by Permission.

To Two Amazing Ladies

Berenice Gilbert, my mother - who has been in heaven since 1997.

&

*Judy Pratt, my sister - a wonderful encourager
who never stopped believing in me.*

Acknowledgments:
Thanks to:

Margaret Smith for editorial insights

Stephanie Berglund for conceptual suggestions and proofing

Amanda Gilliam cover design

Contents

Title Page	1
Copyright	2
Dedication	5
Epigraph	6
Let me Introduce You...	13
Chapter 1 – Learning God's Voice	19
Chapter 2 – Will God Speak To Me?	27
Chapter 3 – How God Speaks	35
Chapter 4 – Discovering Intimacy with God	49
Chapter 5 – Discovering Intimacy Though Partnership	57
Chapter 6 – Discovering Guidance	65
Chapter 7 – Familiarity with the Voice of the Lord	77
Chapter 8 – Listening Beyond Hearing	85
Chapter 9 – Hearing Loss	95
Chapter 10 – Positioning Yourself to Hear	105
Chapter 11 – Humility - The Secret to Hearing	115
Chapter 12 – Soaking in the Presence	127
Chapter 13 – Hearing for the Sake of Encouraging Others	139
Concluding Thoughts...	147
Intimacy Through Hearing	151

End Notes	159
Works Cited	163
About The Author	167
Books By This Author	169

Let me Introduce You...

The present looks different from the past. The idea of going forward in the future feels unclear. In this time of uncertainty - on all fronts - people find themselves stuck. I am writing to believers who many would describe as mature and seasoned. Behind the scenes where no one sees or knows, these believers are stuck. Stuck with the way things have always been. Stuck with the doubt that things can change and not sure of what needs to change, and even if things could change, they find themselves too exhausted to believe that positive change could happen. Or they doubt that they are the ones who really need to change because they know they are going to heaven and after all isn't that all that counts? Saved and satisfied - what could be better?

Some believers have a good knowledge of God's Word, they have security and satisfaction with what they know. They have a lot of answers and opinions that were primarily formed because of what other teachers, pastors and writers have said, but they know little of firsthand revelation directly from the Holy Spirit and doubt that such revelation exists anymore. We can hear their words in our heads: "After all we have the Bible. Isn't that all we need?" This believer will say that a person hearing directly from God is a dangerous precedent. As a result, they accept their present spiritual state and know little of the intimacy of hearing God's voice. Knowledge is the primary fruit of their *dead but don't know it* relationship with God.

Others know precious little of the Scripture and live in a religious environment, hoping their less than stellar knowledge is never found out. Their lives are stuck because their fellowship with God and others is surface and they work hard to keep it that way. They live in embarrassment and unworthiness afraid they can never find intimacy with God because the paradigm they have been taught conveyed that closeness with God is based solely on spiritual knowledge so they have a *defeated and don't know it* relationship with God.

Many have not had a fresh encounter or fresh word from God for so long that they are way past the "fake it until you make it" refrain. They quietly fear the days ahead, unable to express their fear - for fear of being "found out." They are not even sure that fresh encounters are real, so they have a *dry and don't know it* kind of faith.

In our heart of hearts, we doubt that God speaks to people much anymore and we privately and sometimes, even among friends, judge the people who say He has spoken to them. We think they are just manipulative. It is true, there are people who speak perhaps too frequently using phrases like "God said" or "God told me." We treat these individuals as weird fanatics who have clearly been deceived and misled. In some cases that may be true, but we never consider that even if it is counterfeit that behavior presupposes something that is true. We do not consider that judgment of them might offend the God who is more intimate with them than He is with us.

The days ahead are going to be more challenging than some of the days of the past and many of our spiritual coping mechanisms are not going to work. I want to suggest in the pages you are about to read that the God of the Bible who spoke to real men and women is the same today and He definitely wants our attention because He wants us to learn to listen to His voice. Going the road with spiritual and prideful knowledge is not going to work. That road will be lonelier than ever in the days ahead.

I understand the spiritually stuck mindsets I have just described.

I have had a little of each of these in me, which is why I know them well. I have sat in services where the Spirit was moving and I watched from the outside because I was filled with doubt. I treated prophecies and experiences of others with contempt. It was easier to judge than to experience for myself. There was the ever present, "what will people think?" thought. I stayed stuck.

I have not enjoyed the times when God offended my mind and my traditions in order to speak to my heart. I have heard from God, but I have placed religious restrictions on Him based on what I have or have not experienced. This is a problem because the Holy Spirit loves to think outside of my box. I had experienced limited crops of spiritual fruit in my life because I only wanted Him to do it my way. In the end, the way to reconcile my lack of intimacy with Him was to deny that He spoke to me. My biggest challenge in my spiritual walk has not been what I have to learn but what I have had to unlearn.

God has my attention. I am not ashamed to say I hear God's voice. Perhaps not conversationally like some claim. Not perfectly and not all of the time. I have learned it is a normal part of the Christian walk to hear God. You can hear God too. He will answer your prayer when you ask to hear Him. Understand it may be in a way you are not expecting, but our God wants to be known.

When I began writing this book, I was awake at 3:30 AM. I was planning to go back to sleep but He spoke, and emphatically said (no not audibly, I've not experienced that) "you could not know Me if I did not want you to." At first, I thought, "that's really true." But the more I have thought of that phrase, it is not only true, it is His invitation. He wants me to know Him. "Yay God! You want me to know you intimately." God wants all of us to know Him in depth and without superficiality.

It is time to see things differently and to hear differently. Instead of just glibly talking about relationship with God, He is inviting us to a close and real relationship with Him! An intimate, life changing, miracle believing, powerful relationship where the Scriptures are living and our hearing is tuned to His frequency. A relationship in which we walk in step with His cadence. When we read Bible stories, we read with the kind of faith that says, "I am going to experience something like that, and I will experience God in that kind of way." I am confident that when we begin to see things differently and tune our spiritual hearing toward intimacy with Him, we will get unstuck spiritually and see a difference in our own lives and make a difference in the lives of others.

I am still learning. I do not have all this stuff nailed down in my life. I practice listening, because for me, listening at all, is an acquired skill. I feel compelled to write what I know and what I am learning and, in some cases, what I think we as God's family still need to learn. It is time to journey into hearing God's voice and experiencing deep unexplainable intimacy with all of the Godhead: Father, Son, and Holy Spirit.

Instead of us talking the talk and not walking the walk. How about we talk less and listen more? Let's listen to His insights and blessing that He wants to impress, impart, and whisper into our spirits? I want to introduce you to *Intimacy Through Hearing*. To a deeper walk with the Abba, Father who is longing to make Himself known to me and you...

Chapter 1 – Learning God's Voice

Hearing His Voice

The abuse started early for Kaye, unthinkably her father trafficked her by offering her up sexually in exchange for favors from his friends. When Kaye was 14, she was desperate to break the cycle of abuse. Right after one of the horrific and devaluing experiences she sat sobbing on the kitchen floor with a knife. As she took in a deep breath in preparation to slit her wrist, she heard a loud, audible, "NO." It was one single word, loud and parental, but Kaye said, "in that moment I felt flooded with peace and comfort. God speaking to me, was the turning point, I sensed God was on my side. I can now stand up to my dad and his friends." Stand up to them she did! Kaye now ministers with compassion and power to victims of sexual abuse.

If there ever was a day when we need to hear the voice of God, it is today. This is a day when we are not sure what sources to believe. These seem to be the days Jesus promised where there would be wars and rumors of war. Political unrest, pandemics and riots are the present reality. We need the calming, comforting, challenging and never-changing voice of God. These are certainly days of prayer, but we need to rethink prayer a bit. In most of our praying we do nearly all of the talking and truly little listening.

Proverbs 8:32-35 (ESV) says, "And now, O sons, listen to Me: blessed are those who keep My ways. Hear instruction and be wise, and do not neglect it. Blessed is the one who *listens* to Me, *watching* daily at My gates, *waiting* beside My doors. For whoever finds Me finds life and obtains favor from the Lord, [emphasis mine]." Those who listen, watch and wait obtain favor, in other words they find intimacy with the Lord.

David had this shift of rethinking prayer in Psalm 143. David starts his prayer "Lord, hear my prayer, listen to my cry for mercy" (Psalm 143:1). In the first several verses David is wanting to make sure that God is hearing him. The shift comes in verse eight where instead of being worried that God is hearing him, David starts to ask, if he is hearing God. "Let me hear of Your unfailing love each morning, for I am trusting You. Show me where to walk, for I give myself to You" (Psalm 143:8). We need this same shift in our lives. Instead of asking if God is hearing us, it is good to ask if we are hearing and listening to God. God has been listening all along, but He very much wants to be heard so He can reveal His heart of intimacy to us.

Most of the time I think Christians think that when God allows us to hear His voice He is only going to give us directions. Giving directions is not God's primary reason in teaching us to hear His voice. Before we can receive and effectively follow directions, we must develop a heart of obedience and refined hearing that is born out of a heart of intimacy with God.

God Reveals His Heart
God so desires to reveal His heart to us that He mercifully tailors His voice and revelation to how in our human weakness we can hear best. He wants us to hear Him as He speaks.

How God speaks is not as important as the fact that God did speak and that He still speaks today. Francis Frangipane in his great book *Spiritual Discernment and the Mind of Christ* wrote:
> When we accept Christ into our hearts, He does not enter simply as a doctrine. No, He enters us a living voice. His Spirit brings conviction and direction; He speaks through dreams, visions, revelation and understanding of the Scripture. He illuminates our hearts, speaking to us of repentance

and the renewal of our soul. He lifts us, reminding us of the faithful promises of God (28).

Giving our hearts to the Lord is the start of a life changing relationship and in any good relationship there is fellowship and communication.

God declares His unchanging character in Malachi 3:6 "For I am the Lord, I do not change." This is also true of Jesus. Hebrews 13:8 says, "Jesus Christ is the same yesterday and today and forever." We quote verses like these without realizing that the God of Moses is my God. The God that related to Peter is the same God that wants to relate to me. What God did He does and what He does He will continue to do, that includes allowing us to hear His voice.

They Knew It Was God
When God spoke in the Scriptures the people knew it was God Who was speaking, and they were sure what He said, and it usually involved the circumstances in which they were involved. Blackaby and King said:

> The method to speak was different from person to person. What is important is:
> - God uniquely spoke to His people.
> - They knew it was God.
> - They knew what He said (74).

God spoke to Bible characters audibly, through a soft whisper, through other people, through a donkey, through circumstances, out of a burning bush, through an angel, and with a sheet being let down from heaven and more. God was so desirous of revealing His heart to men that He spoke in many ways. He spoke so they knew it was Him and knew what He said and what He wanted them to do because of what was said. They knew it was God's voice because in most of the cases where God spoke there was a close relationship.

Samuel was faithful with every word that God spoke to his heart, even when the words were difficult - when they were delivered to the leaders of Samuel's day (Eli and Saul). No wonder the Bible says, "The Lord was with Samuel as he grew up, and He let none of Samuel's word fall to the ground" (1 Samuel 3:19).

Noah was the builder and God was the architect and vision caster for the biggest building project up to that time in history. God spoke to Noah about the greatest architectural marvel of his day. God clearly trusted Noah in order to entrust such a big and long-term project as the ark. Genesis 6:8 says, "Noah found grace in the eyes of the Lord." To receive such intricate guidance and direction, Noah no doubt had an intimate relationship with the Lord.

Elijah had a willing heart to go where God told him to go, to say what God told him to say and to do what he was told to do. No wonder Elijah had learned to hear God's whisper. He learned to listen to God's voice at a dried-up ravine while being fed by ravens (see 1 Kings 17:2-6). Not many of us would stand in line for that assignment.

Jesus and His Disciples
In the Gospels the disciples had grown accustomed to hearing Jesus' physical voice. He repeatedly prepared them for the day He would go away and no longer be a physical presence, but not to worry they would hear from the Holy Spirit. In John 14:26 (NKJV) He said, "But the Helper, the Holy Spirit, whom the Father will send in My name, He will teach you all things, and bring to your remembrance all things that I said to you." After the resurrection Jesus brought them into a fuller measure of relationship when He breathed on them and said, "receive the Holy Spirit" (see John 20:21-22). These followers were now experiencing saving faith and the saving power of the cross. Jesus was preparing them to fellowship and communicate with Him through the presence, power, and voice of the Holy Spirit.

Jesus promised His disciples that they should expect to hear God speak through the Holy Spirit. The disciples were troubled as they were about to lose His physical presence, He was about to leave them and go back to the splendors of heaven seated at the right hand of His Father. He told them not to worry "'I tell you the truth. It is to your advantage that I go away; for if I do not go away, the Helper will not come to you; but if I depart, I will send Him to you'" (John 16:7 NKJV).

In the forty-day period following His resurrection, while He appeared to them in visible form, He was preparing them for life through the Holy Spirit without His visible presence.
Dallas Willard says:
> His main task as their teacher during these days was to accustom them to hearing Him without seeing Him. Thus, it was "through the Holy Spirit" that He gave instructions to His apostles during this period (Acts 1: 2). He made himself visible to them just enough to give them confidence that it was He Who was speaking in their hearts. This prepared them to continue their conversation with Him after He no longer appeared to them visibly (287).

When they were baptized in the Holy Spirit at Pentecost the disciples had a fuller revelation of all that Jesus said in preparing them to take the Gospel to the ends of the earth and to listen to the Spirit's leading. Jesus was preparing them to learn to hear the voice of God through the Holy Spirit. The Lord always wants to prepare our hearts to hear the voice of God through the Holy Spirit.

God's voice reveals His heart and His character. He desires fellowship with us. He desires to be known by us. He desires us to hear Him. He wants us to know Him.

Points to Ponder
What change does it make in your thinking to understand that God will tailor how He speaks to the way you can best understand

and get His message?

Read through Psalm 143 to see David's shift from being concerned that God was hearing him to being worried that he was hearing God? Ask God if there is a shift you need to make in order to hear Him better.

Prayer Focus: *Lord, I ask your forgiveness that my prayer life has been with me doing most of the talking. Help me to learn to be a better listener that I might hear Your voice better.*

Chapter 2 – Will God Speak To Me?

Hearing His Voice

My friend Evette had an experience with the voice of the Lord she will not soon forget. At the time she and her husband lived in a rural area of Montana. Fond of lovely flower arrangements, she was gathering stocks of wheat for an arrangement. As she was reaching to cut some stocks of wheat, she clearly heard the words "STOP, step back!" As she obeyed the unmistakable voice, she saw a rattlesnake curled beneath the stock of wheat.

God spoke in the Bible times, but does He still speak? More importantly will He speak to me? The answer to this question is an unequivocal yes! I have a notebook where I journal words I hear from God, Scriptures that the Holy Spirit makes come alive to me and dreams that I believe have a message for me from God. I recently heard my friend, April Crider, teaching on dreams and at the end of her excellent teaching she prayed that dreams would be released in the lives of the people she was teaching. That night I had three rather specific dreams. I awoke at 3:30 AM and wanted to write them down before I forgot them. I had misplaced my notebook where I journal these things and was heart sick as I had not seen it for at least three weeks. I thought to myself "I will type them on my phone and if I find my journal, I'll transfer…." I had not and did not pray about it, but before the thought was even completed in my mind, I heard the words,

"Look in the pantry." My first thought upon hearing those words was "why would it be in the pantry?" But what I had heard was so clear, I went straight to the pantry and walked right to my journal. I recorded the three dreams, but in retrospect I am not sure the dreams were the lesson but the message God wanted me to hear. In living in intimacy, we find He cares about the smallest details of our lives.

Some do not think we can hear from God perhaps for a couple of reasons. First, we have heard people use something they say God told them for the purpose of manipulation or to excess, so in rejecting their methodology we also reject that God might want to speak to us. Second, some think that God has already spoken and does not need to speak another word, as He has already spoken through His Word, the Scripture. Indeed, God has already spoken through the Bible but the Scripture itself confirms the continued voice of the Holy Spirit as God relates to His children who are in relationship with Him. Every believer has heard from God. Every true child of God has already heard God speak, for most of us His voice was not audible, but God has spoken. It would be impossible to come to know Christ as our Savior without hearing God's voice.

He Calls Us To Himself
Rick, a relatively new part of our church stood shaking his head with another man with whom he was in a heated discussion. I had yet to meet the other man. I could overhear the impassioned and awkward conversation while I anxiously greeted other guests and attenders as they were leaving the service that bright sunny California day. I prayed no one was noticing or hearing Rick and the other man, although I didn't know how anyone could help but hear them.

The other man visibly angry, growled at Rick, "You told him!"

"I didn't, I swear to it." Rick protested.

This went on for several minutes until Rick pulled the red-faced fellow toward me, "Tell him, Pastor."

I cautiously asked, "What do you want me to tell him?"

Rick said, "Pastor this is my brother in law Larry, you've got to tell him that I never talked to you about him or told you anything that was going on in his life."

I said, "Good to meet you Larry, no I don't believe that Rick has never mentioned you to me."

I explained to Larry, that this kind of thing happens when we feel our private life and sin is being exposed. The reason it happens is God is calling us to come to Jesus so He can forgive our sins and start us on the journey of a wonderful relationship with God. The next Sunday Larry brought his wife Judy to church and again the Spirit of God spoke to them and they wondrously gave their hearts to the Lord.

Many of us have had the experience of attending church or attending a small group Bible study or even a conversation with a good friend and it was as if the pastor, speaker, or friend had been reading our mail. Perhaps we heard a message that stirred something in our hearts and an invitation was given to allow Jesus to become the Lord of our hearts. There was something inside of us saying, "Yes do it" but we were holding on to the seat in front with white knuckles out of fear of the unknown or even the fear of what others would think. That is what is often called conviction, a loving God is persuading us that He loves us and will forgive our sins. We could not be saved without the Spirit of God speaking to us and calling us into relationship with God.

The Bible indicates that when God calls us, He does so not only so we can be forgiven but so that we can step into intimacy with Him. There are many passages of Scripture that point to this fact, for example Revelation 22:17 (AMPC) says:

> The [Holy] Spirit and the bride (the church, the true Christians) say, Come! And let him who is listening say, Come! And

let everyone come who is thirsty [who is painfully conscious of his need of those things by which the soul is refreshed, supported, and strengthened]; and whoever [earnestly] desires to do it, let him come, take, appropriate, and drink the water of Life without cost.

The Spirit says "come." The bride of Christ says "come." The verse includes a third invite "Let him who is listening say, Come!" Scholars are not clear on who the third invitation is from. I very much believe Abba Father is listening and He also longs for us to come. It is His delight for us to come. When we come there is a major party in heaven. Abba God loves to throw parties on our behalf, He loves us that much. These celebrations are mentioned in Luke 15. Luke 15:10 (TPT) says, "…every time one lost sinner repents and turns to Him. He says to all his angels, 'Let's have a joyous celebration, for that one who was lost I have found!'"

He Speaks Assurance To Our Hearts
After we give our hearts to the Lord, the Bible says that this same Spirit witnesses, or testifies, to our spirit that we are a child of God. Romans 8:16 TPT says, "For the Holy Spirit makes God's fatherhood real to us as He whispers into our innermost being, 'You are God's beloved child!'" When we give our hearts to the Lord, the intimate Holy Spirit wants to bring the comfort that we know what we have experienced is true. He testifies that we are God's child.

The Holy Spirit is also called an Advocate. John 15:26 says, "When the Advocate comes, Whom I will send to you from the Father—the Spirit of truth who goes out from the Father—He will testify about Me." Advocate and testify are both legal terms. When someone gives a testimony in court, they are sworn to tell the truth. When the Holy Spirit testifies or whispers to you "you are a child of God," He is sworn to tell the truth.

This assurance to our hearts is also confirmed in John 10:2-5:
> The one who enters by the gate is the shepherd of the sheep. The gatekeeper opens the gate for Him, and the sheep

listen to His voice. He calls His own sheep by name and leads them out. When He has brought out all His own, He goes on ahead of them, and His sheep follow Him because they know His voice. But they will never follow a stranger; in fact, they will run away from him because they do not recognize a stranger's voice.

The loving protection of the Father is seen in this passage. God is all about protecting all those who belong to Him. He opens the gate for the Good Shepherd so that He can lead His sheep to still waters and green pastures. The Shepherd leads them by going ahead of them to spot any predators and pitfalls, and with His tender voice bids them to follow.

Because the sheep belong to Him, He calls them by name, so they cannot mistake that He is talking to them. Samuel finally knew that it was God speaking to him because God called him by his name. He called Saul by name. He called Mary Magdalene by name at the resurrection. Be assured He who knows their names also knows you by name and wants to communicate with you in a most personal way.

Will God Speak To Me?
God intends to speak to us. If He planned to be aloof and silent, unquestionably He would not have spoken so often regarding our hearing. Jeremiah 33:3 says, "Call to Me and I will answer you and tell you great and unsearchable things you do not know." The Bible uses the expression "let him who has ears, hear" at least fifteen times. God clearly desires to speak to His children. I am sure I have missed many things God has said to me, through my preoccupation with the things of life or through my inability to recognize His voice. God is ready to speak so we should prepare our hearts and minds to hear and live in anticipation and a posture of listening to hear what He has to say.

∞∞∞

Points to Ponder
Romans 8:16 (TPT) says, "For the Holy Spirit makes God's fatherhood real to us as He whispers into our innermost being, 'You are God's beloved child!'" In what ways have your experienced that?

What steps can you take this week to recognize God's voice? Take some time to study John 10 and what Jesus says about His sheep.

A word of discernment relative to God's calling (conviction), this tug at our heart, to come into a right relationship with God through what Jesus did for us on the cross: The voice of God is not a voice of condemnation. God's heart is not to judge or condemn, but to lead us into a new direction. God not only removes our sins, He forgets them. Isaiah 43:25 (NLT) says, "I—yes, I alone —will blot out your sins for My own sake and will never think of them again." After this process the guilt is gone, so if you still feel guilty it is not guilt because the guilt is paid in full. It is guilt feelings. The enemy preys on this as he wants us to doubt our salvation. It is Satan's voice that brings condemnation. Romans 8:1 says, "there is now no condemnation for those who are in Christ Jesus."

Because God has forgotten our confessed sins, it is neither helpful nor spiritually beneficial to keep on confessing. Confessing and re-confessing the same thing is like trying to pay for something already paid for - repeatedly. A little tool that has been helpful to me:
1. Stop
2. Think (Yes! I have been forgiven)
3. Thank (Thank You Lord, for Your wonderous forgiveness).

Prayer Focus: *Lord help me regularly expect to hear from You. Make Your Word come alive and speak to my heart as I read it. But also, help me to tune into Your voice throughout the day in anticipation of the fact that You desire to speak to me.*

Chapter 3 – How God Speaks

Hearing His Voice

Catherine of Siena, (Italian Saint 1347-1380), at one time spent three days in a solitary retreat, praying for a greater fullness of joy of the Divine presence. Instead of this, it seemed as though legions of wicked spirits assailed her with blasphemous thoughts and even suggestions. At length, a great light appears to descend from above. The devils fled, and the Lord Jesus conversed with her, Catherine asked Him: "Lord, where wert Thou when my heart was so tormented?"

"I was in thy heart," He answered.

"O Lord, Thou art everlasting truth," she replied, "and I humbly bow before Thy word; but how can I believe that Thou wast in my heart when it was filled with such detestable thoughts?"

"Did these thoughts give thee pleasure or pain?" He asked.

"An exceeding pain and sadness," was her reply.

To whom the Lord said, "Thou wast in woe and sadness because I was in the midst of thy heart. My presence it was which rendered those thoughts insupportable to thee. When the period I had determined for the duration of the combat had elapsed, I sent forth the beam of My light, and the shades of hell were dispelled, because they cannot resist that light" (Meyer, 21-22).

God spoke in the Bible times, and He still speaks. How can you expect He will speak to you? God loves you so much and desires to be known by you He will speak in many and varied ways so you can best hear Him. Here are some primary ways He speaks and availing yourself to these will help you develop your spiritual ears to hear His voice more frequently.

He Speaks Through His Word
The primary way in which God speaks is His Word, the Bible. All other forms of hearing must be discerned and held up against the standard of Scripture. Peter said, the Scriptures are completely reliable, and we do well as we pay attention (see 2 Peter 1:19). The Word is an expression of the heart of Jesus from the beginning (see John 1:1). Unlike any other book, the Scripture is living, which means as we read, the Holy Spirit applies it to our hearts. Which is why when you read the Bible one time you can see and receive something deeper and different than at another time. The Holy Spirit knows how to appropriate the Word according to what is happening in your life at the moment, which is why Hebrews 4:12 says, "For the word of God is alive and active. Sharper than any double-edged sword, it penetrates even to dividing soul and spirit, joints and marrow; it judges the thoughts and attitudes of the heart."

Paul said to Timothy, "All Scripture is God-breathed and is useful for teaching, rebuking, correcting and training in righteousness, so that the servant of God may be thoroughly equipped for every good work" (see 2 Timothy 3:16-17). "Teaching" shows us the path we are to walk for our lives. "Rebuking" speaks to us when we fall off or step off the path. "Correcting" is God loving us to provide instruction on how to get back on the path so we may continue our journey. "Training" speaks to us about how to stay on the path and keep moving forward in fellowship with Christ. The Holy Spirit uses the Scripture to equip you for a victorious life.

There two are common words used in the Greek language for the term "word". The term used most often is *logos*. The words printed on a page are *logos*. When I am reading the Bible, I am reading *logos*. The word *logos* is used over 300 times in the New Testament. The second term is *rhema* which refers to a freshly spoken word. *Rhema* is used over seventy times. When we are reading the *logos* (written word) and it jumps off the page and speaks to a specific area of my life, the *logos* becomes *rhema* (a freshly spoken word). In Matthew 4:4 (NKJV) as Jesus was countering Satan's lie with Scripture, He said (quoting from Deuteronomy 8:3): "It is written, 'Man shall not live by bread alone, but by every word that proceeds from the mouth of God.'" In commenting on the Greek tense James Goll says:

> Proceeds is a continuous-action verb. God's life-giving word proceeds and continues to proceed. It is God's ever-proceeding word that gives us life! God has spoken; God is speaking; God will continue to guide His children by speaking (44).

God wants His written word to speak to your heart in specific ways so that it is fresh and transforming. Priscilla Shirer in her helpful book *Discerning the Voice of God* is describing *rhema* when she writes:

> As you seek to hear the Holy Spirit speak through Scripture, you are tuning your spiritual ears to catch that moment when a passage, verse, phrase or even just a single word grasps your attention in an almost shocking way, drawing your thoughts directly toward it and how it applies to a specific situation in your life (87).

Once I understand the Word is alive, I can come to times of reading with expectation and my ears and my mind in a teachable mode to hear and understand what the Lord wants to teach and tell me. C.H. Spurgeon said, "The Bible is the heart of God made legible" (Behold Your God 53).

Henri Nouwen, an expert in spiritual formations, speaks of the mistake of treating the Bible just like any other book, when he says:

> It helps to realize that the Bible is not primarily a book of information about God but of formation of the heart. It is not merely a book to be analyzed, scrutinized, and discussed, but a book to nurture, unify, and serve as a constant source of contemplation. We must struggle constantly against the temptation to read the Bible instrumentally as a book full of

> good stories and illustrations...The Bible does not speak to us as long as we want to use it...Only when we are willing to hear the written word as a word for us can the Living Word disclose Himself and penetrate into the center of our heart (93).

It is easy to get into a rut with devotions or quiet time and come to the Scripture looking at it only as a written word. There is nothing wrong with reading long passages of Scripture and attempting to read the Bible through every year. But there is a danger in just trying to check the proverbial "I read it" box without taking the time to let it come alive in our hearts. When we read this way, it leaves us unchanged.

Romans 10:17 says, "Consequently, faith comes from hearing the message, and the message is heard through the word about Christ." James Goll says,

> The word for hearing means to have audience with, to come with ears...If we approach the Word of God with the correct inner attitude of the heart, by coming with ears ready to listen, we will give full attention to the Word, have an audience with it and leave changed (73).

God wants to fellowship with you and speak to you and one of those primary ways is through the Scripture. As we see our time with the Scripture as fellowship with God we can allow Him to massage, impress, imbed and speak its meaning into our hearts and minds. It is wonderful the thoughts and impressions that come into our hearts in this way.

One of my favorite questions is "Holy Spirt what does this mean?" He not only loves to answer, He loves to teach. This truth is shared in John 16:13, "But when He, the Spirit of truth, comes, He will guide you into all the truth. He will not speak on His own; He will speak only what He hears, and He will tell you what is yet to come." The Scriptures will come alive in us and a *rhema* (a fresh word) will be revealed in the hearts of believers who are hungry for God's work in their lives.

The focus of Psalm 119, the longest chapter in the Bible, is resplendent with the benefits of the Word to our lives. One of the most familiar is verse Psalm 119:11, "Your word I have hidden in my heart, That I might not sin against You." Again, James Goll has a great observation:

> There is a direct correlation between hearing and hiding the Word of God in our heart and mind...To the degree we actively hide the Word of God in our soul, we can expect to hear the revelatory, or spoken word of God resounding in our heart. Hiding and hearing are divinely connected! (71).

Hiding the Word in our hearts takes time and there is also a connection between the time we spend not just in reading, but in reading to listen to what God wants to say.

As you read the Scripture cherish and ponder it. Come expecting it to be a personal word to your life. Scripture is the primary way God speaks, it is not the only way God speaks, but it "provides the boundaries into which everything else He says to you will fall" (Priscilla Shirer 86).

He Speaks Through People

God frequently speaks to us through another person. Sometimes it is a word of encouragement the Lord lays on their heart to give to us. Other times it may be a prophetic word. New Testament prophetic words are defined in 1 Corinthians 14:3 "But the one who prophesies speaks to people for their strengthening, encouraging and comfort." So prophecy is used to build up, stir up and cheer up another person as the Lord leads. Prophetic author, Kris Vallotton says, "The prophetic ministry actually calls forth the image and likeness of God in someone. When we prophesy, people come into awareness of original glory" (54). God uses people to call out the best in us - consistent with the Scripture.

Two years ago, someone sent me a text message with John 7:37-39 and said, "The Lord impressed me to share this verse with you." I do not often write those things down, but in the case, I am glad I did. Six months, later I was handed a note card, with John 7:37-39 written on it, and the person who gave it to me said, I believe I was supposed to give this to you. A year later I was at a conference and in an extremely specific way the speaker prophetically identified me (we had not met) and said, "I am hearing John 7:37-39 over your life." It was a special moment where I sensed God's presence in a powerful way. I had forgotten about the text and the note card, which had the very same passage of Scripture. When I put together these three separate events it reminded me of 2 Corinthians 13:1 "Every matter must be established by the testimony of two or three witnesses." (This passage is also found in Deuteronomy 19:15 and Matthew 18:16). I have no doubt God really wants me to hear His voice relative to John 7:37-39:

> On the last and greatest day of the festival, Jesus stood and said in a loud voice, 'Let anyone who is thirsty come to Me and drink. Whoever believes in me, as Scripture has said, rivers of living water will flow from within them.' By this He meant the Spirit, whom those who believed in Him were later to receive.

I have memorized and am meditating on it as I want to receive every bit of revelation, He has for me on this passage. He used different people to deliver the same message to me.

Most believers know the Scripture,"Do not quench the Holy Spirit." The very next verse has another important and I believe equal command, "Do not treat prophecies with contempt." Paul qualifies this command however, when he said, "but test them all; hold on to what is good" (see 1 Thessalonians 5:19-21). Great advice. All prophecy given to you by other people must be consistent with the Scripture. If it is not in line with the Scripture, reject it and move on.

He Speaks in a Whisper
God is not like the exasperated mother in the big box store continually raising her voice at her children to no avail. The kids

have grown so used to the decibel level they no longer hear. God is typically not a yeller. In most situations He will not compete with the noise of your life. Noise disrupts our prayers often. Silencing our phones is a good practice. It is not just outside noises, A J Sherrill in his great little book *Quiet* says, "the inner noise of the mind can be just as loud as the sirens on my street, and this inner noise is harder to shake than taking a train ride out of the city" (9). We miss intimacy with God due to both the noise from within and from without.

As mentioned earlier Elijah learned to the hear God at Kerith Brook as he was fed by ravens. Kerith would not be Elijah's last lesson in hearing God. 1 Kings 19:11-13 says:

> The Lord said, 'Go out and stand on the mountain in the presence of the Lord, for the Lord is about to pass by.' Then a great and powerful wind tore the mountains apart and shattered the rocks before the Lord, but the Lord was not in the wind. After the wind there was an earthquake, but the Lord was not in the earthquake. After the earthquake came a fire, but the Lord was not in the fire. And after the fire came a gentle whisper. When Elijah heard it, he pulled his cloak over his face and went out and stood at the mouth of the cave.

We have all heard amazing testimonies of God speaking in a powerful way. Those kinds of experiences are more exceptional than normal. Ask God to help you learn, like Elijah, to hear His whispers.

Mark Batterson, Pastor of National Community Church in Washington DC, in his great book *Whisper* says, "The Almighty could intimidate us with His outside voice, but He woos us with a whisper" (10). Batterson continues, "Nothing has the potential to change your life like the whisper of God. Nothing will determine your destiny more than your ability to hear His still small voice" (11). Little is as intimate as someone leaning close to us to whisper something in our ear. God desires us to lean into Him to hear His whispers.

When our son was born, like most babies he did not sleep through the night at first. I am now embarrassed to say I slept through some of those diaper changes and bottle feedings in the wee hours of the morning. Unlike me, my wife's ear was tuned to his cry and the sounds of his whimper. I want to be so tuned to God's voice that I do not miss one whisper, one impression, one God thought.

He Speaks in Our Thoughts
While God's voice is seldom audible, we may hear Him through our thoughts. It is subtle and most of the time when God speaks in our thoughts it is more like we realize something. We realize or think something we would not normally think. We think something that we are not smart enough to think by ourselves. Dallas Willard says:

> There are times that a soft still voice accompanies our thoughts. "still, small voice—or the interior or inner voice, as it is also called—is the preferred and most valuable form of individual communication for God's purposes. God usually addresses individually those who walk with Him in a mature, personal relationship using this inner voice (118).

The thought might feel like an impression providing us necessary direction, guidance, or information, but it is unmistakable that it came from God.

There are times during prayer or a time of quiet that a name or a situation is impressed on our hearts. The impression may be slight, but we must be careful to listen, God may have an important word of encouragement for someone and He has chosen us to deliver the message. Or there are times that a name is impressed on our hearts without our knowing the reason, consider that a call to commence praying for that person. We should seek the mind of the Spirit to begin interceding for the person brought to mind. A person's name is never just placed in our minds coincidentally or without purpose.

He Speaks Through Circumstances

God offers guidance and communicates with us through open and closed doors. As mentioned earlier God used this method of communication with the Apostle Paul. Acts 16:6-10 records that as Paul and his companions were seeking to go into Asia, they were kept by the Holy Spirit from preaching there. When they came to the border of Mysia and Bithynia, they were kept from entering both places. It is a good thing or Paul might not have seen the vision where he heard a man from Macedonia calling him to come. And what a fruitful ministry he had in Macedonia. It is through open and closed doors that we have books in the Bible such as Thessalonians and Philippians, all the results of ministry fruit in Macedonia.

When circumstances change and doors close, let us not miss the opportunity by getting wrapped up in disappointment. Listen and look to see how God seems to be moving and flowing and be ready to the step into the next opportunity. As we mature in our walk with the Lord, we learn more and more to appreciate divine appointments but also divine timing.

In our journey with Jesus there are many things that a non-discerning person might describe as coincidental. Unexpected meetings or conversations with an old friend or a new acquaintance have often been orchestrated by the Holy Spirit to open a door or to bring information. Some of these "arranged by the Holy Spirit" meetings are also to set up the groundwork for some blessing yet to come. We can trust God in our circumstances, He is often speaking to us out of them.

God Speaks During Prayer

Many fail to understand God speaks through prayer because we think that when we are done talking the prayer time is over. A quick "Amen" and we are done. That is when the prayer time is just getting started. If we are talking and not still and listening we will not know God's voice through prayer. In the classic *The Prac-*

tice of the Presence of God, Brother Lawrence says:
> My friend says that by dwelling in the presence of God he has established such a sweet communion with the Lord that his spirit abides, without much effort, in the restful peace of God. In this center of rest, he is filled with a faith that equips him to handle anything that comes into his life (475 of 710 Kindle Version).

Prayer is not a one-way form of communication with us doing most of the talking. The Bible has much to say about our listening and waiting and being still before God.

When we pray we should keep our Bibles available. God uses the Scripture in tandem with prayer. *Experiencing God* says: "When I pray about something, Scripture often comes to my mind. I don't see it as a distraction. I believe He is trying to guide me through the Scripture" (88). When this happens, we should stop talking and start listening to what He wants to say to us through the Word.

We really need to rethink prayer. In our noisy world we have grown uncomfortable with stillness and quiet. Our prayer times typically have too much time with us talking and too little time with us listening for Him to speak. Psalm 46:10 says, "Be still, and know that I am God." If we are to hear, we must listen. This will take time and practice and the understanding this is a huge part of praying.

May our prayer times be a place of placing our needs before God, but then listening for His comfort and direction.

He Speaks in Our Sleep and Dreams
Dreams and whispers in the night are one of the most underestimated ways in which God speaks. There is story after story about how God is using dreams in far away places that do not have the Word of God in print to reveal Himself and His love to people who maybe have never heard the name of Jesus. Dreams may well be one of the primary ways God speaks to and calls the lost during

the end of days.

Many believers do not take their dreams seriously and underestimate that this is one of the ways that God speaks. David said, "I will praise the Lord, who counsels me; even at night my heart instructs me" (Psalm 16:7). As I mentioned before, I have a journal where I write down words and dreams I believe are from God. This began several years ago when I decided to start taking my dreams seriously by writing my dreams down upon getting out of bed. I discovered God was speaking to me in imagery, symbols, and through the words of my dreams. I am positive now that I have missed many things that God wanted to say and reveal to me because I was discounting this form of speaking. I do not believe that every dream I have is God speaking to me, but over the last years there have been some unmistakable dreams where God gave a message or warning that I needed to navigate through some of the storms of my life. Job 33:14-18 says:

> For God does speak—now one way, now another—though no one perceives it. In a dream, in a vision of the night, when deep sleep falls on people as they slumber in their beds, He may speak in their ears and terrify them with warnings, to turn them from wrongdoing and keep them from pride, to preserve them from the pit, their lives from perishing by the sword.

Daniel, Joseph and Jacob all had revelatory messages through dreams, but they are not the only ones, so do I. So can you.

He Speaks Through Creation
Psalm 19:1 says, "The heavens declare the glory of God; the skies proclaim the work of His hands." The vastness of space and the complexity of nature testify to God's love for mankind and His magnificence. Go into nature often, observe of what Isaiah spoke, "You will go out in joy and be led forth in peace; the mountains and hills will burst into song before you, and all the trees of the field will clap their hands" (see Isaiah 55:12). Join in the song, raise your voice and hands in praise. Listen to the creek, the songs

of birds, listen to the stillness and the wind whistling through the trees. In that moment of observing grandeur ask, "Holy Spirit, what do You want me to hear?" The quietness of creation speaks so loudly that Paul says, "For since the creation of the world God's invisible qualities—His eternal power and divine nature—have been clearly seen, being understood from what has been made, so that people are without excuse" (Romans 1:20).

These eight ways God speaks are not meant as an exhaustive list. God has many ways of speaking. We can learn to make ourselves available to the Word, to prayer, listening to others, tuning into dreams and hiking through and observing creation. These are great ways to posture ourselves to hear. We need to ask God to give us a greater hunger to be in His presence and ask Him to give us listening ears to hear. Do not rush, we have been invited into a place of greatest privilege, the place of hearing God.

∞∞∞

Points to Ponder
As you read the Scripture read it in context and ask good questions of biblical interpretation. For example, when was this book, chapter, verse, written? Who was it written to and what was the cultural context? What was the writer saying to the audience? And then, here is where it comes alive, ask, "Holy Spirit, what do you want me to do as a result of this passage?"

Consider keeping a dream notebook. Writing down your dreams right after the dream happens or first thing in the morning is a good practice. Then ask the Lord, is there something You are saying to me through this dream?

Focus for Prayer: *Father, I thank You that You find many ways to communicate with Your children. I praise You that You will speak to me in a way that enables me to best hear You.*

Chapter 4 – Discovering Intimacy with God

Hearing His Voice

My friend Lynn D. was hospitalized with the Covid-19 virus. Lynn writes, "I was in a sealed room in isolation. Someone would come in every few hours to take vitals. I could not hear a word they were saying due to their many masks. I started to feel fear creep in. So, I started praying, I heard or felt no response for hours. Then I decided to beg God that I would feel His presence with me. I was just praying in the spirit and I heard Him speak. I felt there was a little frustration with me from our Lord which got my attention; then I heard loud and clear: 'NO, I do not have to let you feel My presence. Does My word not say, I will NEVER leave you or forsake you? My word is true. Trust it! It is My word. Walk by faith, little one. I am with you. You can believe what I say to you. I am with you forever. Rest in Me. Don't grow weary.' I immediately knew God was really speaking to me. Then for the rest of the night I lay there and time after time remembered the numerous times God had spoken to me how He had worked out in so many situations in my life."

When God speaks His primary purpose is always to reveal more of His nature and character to us. While He gives direction, most importantly, He wants to reveal Himself to us. He wants relationship with us. He wants us to know Him. The moment we are born again eternal life starts. All of eternity will be daily discoveries of something fresh from our Heavenly Father. He desires such closeness with us, that He wants these discoveries to start right now. John 17:3 says: "Now this is eternal life: that they know You, the only true God, and Jesus Christ, Whom You have sent."

It would be impossible to know God if He did not want to be known. The thought that we, mere humans, were created for fellowship and intimacy with the God of the universe stretches our minds to new dimensions.

Intimacy is defined as close familiarity in a deep friendship. In any relationship, intimacy requires trust and safety to feel free enough to let go of ourselves to be known by another. Unlike intimacy in other relationships, the relationship with God is different in that He already knows us better than we even know ourselves. He knows us and loves us so this relationship grows through God making Himself known to us and by our receiving and delighting in this revelation of intimacy. Every day there is something new and different to learn about Him as our awareness of Him deepens. He is so immense it will take all of eternity to grasp how wide and long and high and deep is the love of Christ (see Ephesians 3:18-19).

In speaking of hearing His voice some writers attempt to give a list of "how to's" and techniques for hearing the Lord's voice. There are tools and tips mentioned in this writing, but it is important to realize all of the tools anyone can provide to us can never take the place of discovering intimacy with Him or the utter delight of spending time with Him. I know of no one who regrets spending time getting to know the heart of God. There is a freshness that comes to our thinking, and our living as a result of being in His presence.

Jesus Modeled Intimacy With the Father
In Mark chapter one we see Jesus healing the sick and delivering demons late into the night (see Mark 1:32-34). After such a busy night most of us would have chosen to sleep in the next morning, but not Jesus. Intimacy with the Father was more important than sleep and or any plans He might have had. The next verse (vs. 35) says that Jesus got up before daylight to go spend time with the Father. The Father loved the time Jesus spent with Him in the mornings. Just as the Father loved to spend time with Jesus He longs to spend time with us. It is so wonderful when we hear Him whisper as we are waking up, asking if we can spend some time together?

Jack Deere in his book *Surprised by the Voice of God*, says: "If we want a deep friendship with God, it is important to cultivate a state of mind where we view all of our time as God's time, a state of mind where we are totally available to Him" (312). A heart available to God at any time is key to not missing His voice. We sometimes miss His voice when He chooses to speak at a time we think is not convenient for us, such as in the middle of the night or at a busy time. Think of it this way, the God of the universe desires our company. For us to even consider our own convenience is unthinkable. Being obsessed with our schedules, our "to do list" and how busy we are, is a sure way to miss the blessing of intimacy. In what we might consider important things, Paul says, "I consider everything a loss because of the surpassing worth of knowing Christ Jesus my Lord, for whose sake I have lost all things. I consider them garbage, that I may gain Christ" (Philippians 3:8).

There is always something of Himself that He wants to show us, whether His character, His purpose, or His heart. We should never pass up an opportunity to learn more about our Heavenly Father. He wants to reveal Himself, not only as Heavenly Father, but as our intimate Father. Three times the Bible uses the affectionate term Abba, like the English word "Papa." "Abba" was one of the first words from the Jewish baby's lips. It was not only easy to say, but a word of intimacy and complete trust.

There was only one occasion in Scripture when Jesus called His Father, "God." Matthew 27:46 says: "About three in the afternoon Jesus cried out in a loud voice, *'Eli, Eli, lema sabachthani?'* which means 'My God, my God, why have you forsaken me?" The moment the One Who knew no sin, became sin for us was the moment He called His Abba "God." When He felt the separation and heavy weight of the sins of the world was the only time He used a less intimate expression in referring to His Father.

In Rabbinical commentaries it was stated that slaves were forbidden to address the head of the family by this title (Vine 1). Only the children of the Father could use Abba. "Abba" is the defining term for father. "Abba" in the Aramaic language, was spoken by Jesus and Paul as an intimate term to characterize their personal relationships with God (Dictionary.com). No wonder Paul says in Romans 8:15-16, "The Spirit you received does not make you slaves, so that you live in fear again; rather, the Spirit you received brought about your adoption to sonship. And by Him we cry, 'Abba, Father.' The Spirit Himself testifies with our spirit that we are God's children."

We are not only called God's children so we can have the intimacy of Papa God, Jesus tells us in John 15:15 (TPT), "I have never called you 'servants,' because a master doesn't confide in his servants, and servants don't always understand what the master is doing. But I call you my most intimate friends, for I reveal to you everything that I've heard from my Father." Think of it, our Abba Father and His Son Jesus desire to confide with us. God has gone to every length to bring us into a relationship with Him, even sending His Son to the cross that we might know what a forgiving Abba (Papa) Father He is and that we might recognize His voice.

Hearing Flows Out of Intimacy With God

James 4:8 (NKJV) says, "Draw near to God and He will draw near to you." Hearing does not happen from a distance. It happens as we come closer and closer into the presence of God. This is the reason, the hunger and heart to hear God is more important than our ability to hear. Seeking to develop some formula for hearing God never works, it is wanting to spend time in His presence that attracts His voice. His voice is heard in intimacy.

We are blessed by what God does for us, through us, and in us. But we must want intimacy with God more than we want what He can do in and for us. We must want Him more than we want to hear His voice. We are familiar with the story in Luke 15:11-21 of the prodigal son. It is full of important truths. Timothy Keller in his amazing book *Prodigal God* aptly points to the fact that there are two sons in the story: not just one, a younger and an elder brother. Keller says, "Elder brothers obey God to get things. They don't obey God to get God Himself - in order to resemble Him, love Him, know Him and delight Him" (49). When we want God's things and blessings more than we want God we will have trouble being close enough to hear God's voice.

Dallas Willard says, "Usually, those who want a word from God when they are in trouble cannot find it. Or at least they have no assurance that they have found it. This is, I think, because they do not first and foremost simply want to hear God speaking in their lives in general" (258). Pursuit of intimacy with God is the surest way to discover His voice. Paul said in Philippians 3:10 in the Amplified Bible Classic Edition:

> [For my determined purpose is] that I may know Him [that I may progressively become more deeply and intimately acquainted with Him, perceiving and recognizing and understanding the wonders of His Person more strongly and more clearly], and that I may in that same way come to know the power outflowing from His resurrection...

To not pursue this deep intimacy with Father God is to relegate your Christian walk to a spirit of religiosity. Isaiah writes of a spirit of religion when God says, "These people come near to me with their mouths and honor me with their lips, but their hearts are far from me" (Isaiah 29:13).

The Holy Spirit Our Intimate Friend.
On a trip to Israel, our guide, Henney had an appealing way about him. "This way my friends," he would kindly and assuredly speak. He was so knowledgeable, but also so mellow that I wanted to follow closely and not miss anything he said. As Henney led us through the Holy Land, his style and demeanor felt sensitive and tender. Much like the Holy Spirit, he was gentle, he kept the group on track and was patient with every question.

The Holy Spirit loves to teach, He loves our questions. As He guides, He also comforts, helps, counsels and advocates (see John 14:16). He is indeed an intimate friend. "When the Holy Spirit leads us, He not only does so persistently, but He also does it personally and individually" (Priscilla Shirer 79).

What an extraordinary gift the Father gave to us when He sent the Holy Spirit to be our Counselor and Helper. He longs for intimacy with us which is why Ephesians 4:30 warns us to "not grieve the Holy Spirit." The Greek word for "grieved" is *lupete*. This word denotes the grief experienced between two people who deeply love each other. It is used in the context of a husband and wife where one of the parties has been unfaithful. One partner has placed their intimacy somewhere outside the bonds of the relationship. The Holy Spirit is most grieved when we fail to take Jesus seriously. He is grieved when we look for intimacy outside of Jesus as it is through intimacy with Jesus, we hear the Lord's voice best.

When we ask a question, we should remember that the time spent in His presence is more important than the answer we are to receive. So, we should not attempt to rush Him. He will be faithful to show us or speak His answer to us. It may take longer than we think that it should. We must not make the mistake of taking the situation into our own hands. Remember when God gives His answer it will be in a way that reveals perfect kingdom timing.

Points to Ponder

What steps can you take to work on your intimacy with God? In what ways would intimacy help you to be able to hear God more effectively?

How would seeking the Father as *Abba* Father influence your relationship with God in a helpful direction? Note: God's title of "Abba Father" is found in the passages of Romans 8:15, Mark 14:36, and Galatians 4:6.

A.W. Tozer said, "the man who would truly know God must give time to Him" (Goodreads). In what ways is this true?

Think about the thought that some want the Father's things more than they want the Father. It is important for each us to check our hearts in this area.

Focus for prayer: *Lord help me to quest for intimacy with you. I want to accept Your promise that as I come near to You, You will come near to me. I desire to be with You Lord and desire to hear Your voice.*

Chapter 5 – Discovering Intimacy Though Partnership

Hearing His Voice

Liz began wearing hearing aids when she was four. In a recent interview Liz said, "I am not less than because I can't hear. I thank Him for this loss of hearing because I desire the gift of hearing and seeing in the spirit more. I have felt the Holy Spirit say to me, 'Liz, your identity is in Me, not in anything else, not your job, your hearing, your kids, your husband. Surrender and be still.' Disappointments have caused me to frequently say, 'God, you are my best friend.' I believe I hear better in the spirit when I affirm that God is my best friend."

What if God asked us to do something really bold? What if God asked us to do something that takes us outside the boundaries of our comfort zone? That is exactly what God did with Ananias. God asked Ananias to go lay hands on Saul for the restoration of his sight and to pray for him. Saul was the most notorious enemy of Christianity of the day. God did not ask Ananias to go without information, He told Ananias that Saul had a miraculous encounter with Jesus and was expecting him.

Ananias wanted to confirm that He was hearing right. "Lord," Ananias answered, "I have heard many reports about this man and all the harm he has done to Your holy people in Jerusalem. And he has come here with authority from the chief priests to arrest all who call on Your name" (Acts 9:13-14). The equivalent would be if God asked us to go pray for and lay hands on a noted terrorist. We would want to make sure we were hearing correctly.

God confirmed that Ananias was hearing correctly. "But the Lord said to Ananias, 'Go! This man is my chosen instrument to proclaim My name to the Gentiles'" (Acts 9:15). God trusted Ananias as a faithful partner in ministry as He had already shown Saul a vision of a man named Ananias coming to the place he was staying.

There are certain blessings we will never know as long as our fear is in control of our lives. If playing it safe is how we operate, we will miss many blessings of being used by God. One of God's primary purposes for speaking to us is to bring us into ministry opportunities. God speaks to people He can trust to carry out a calling and task with obedience.

Ananias headed to the given address on Straight Street. He must have been nervous with sweaty palms, but his obedience to the voice of God would override his human responses. The story continues, in Acts 19:17-18:

> Then Ananias went to the house and entered it. Placing his hands on Saul, he said, 'Brother Saul, the Lord—Jesus, who appeared to you on the road as you were coming here—has sent me so that you may see again and be filled with the Holy Spirit.' Immediately, something like scales fell from Saul's eyes, and he could see again. He got up and was baptized.

Such an amazing outcome did not just happen. In all likelihood Ananias had an intimate relationship with the Holy Spirit and had been practicing his spiritual hearing for some time. He had proved faithful in small things to be used for such an important assignment.

His Plans and Our Partnership Revealed

One of the great mysteries and miracles of the kingdom is that God takes common ordinary people who are faithful and uses them in partnership for accomplishing His purposes and plans on earth. "When He is about to do something, He takes the initiative and comes to one or more of His servants. He lets them know what He is about to do. He invites them to adjust their lives to Him, so He can accomplish His work through them" (Blackaby and King 65). If it is something that we can accomplish in our own strength without God's help, be cautious; that may not be God's voice. Just as Ananias had to trust God for a task beyond His own ability, when God calls us into partnership with Him it will stretch us and make demands of us that will require the supernatural strength of the Lord.

God does not reveal His plan just for our information, He reveals His plan so that we can join Him in what He is doing. Jesus modeled this for us. "Very truly I tell you, the Son can do nothing by Himself; He can do only what He sees His Father doing, because whatever the Father does the Son also does" (John 5:19).

Dallas Willard indicates that there is an intimacy with God in this partnership. "God wants us to understand through immersion with Him in His work. We understand what He is doing so well that we often know exactly what He is thinking and intending to do" (71). The prophet Amos indicated that "Surely the Sovereign Lord does nothing without revealing His plan to His servants the prophets" (Amos 3:7). God confides in His faithful followers.

God reveals and partners with people that He can trust. Jesus gave us a parable regarding this, in Matthew 25. In the story the master went on a journey and left his gold with three of his servants to manage. To one he gave five bags, to another three and to yet another he gave one. He gave according to their ability to manage the gold, so it appears this is not the first time the master has entrusted his gold to his servants. To the trustworthy servants he said, "Well done, my good and faithful servant. You have been faithful in handling this small amount, so now I will give you many more responsibilities. Let's celebrate together!" (Matthew 25:23). In our spiritual immaturity we sometimes doubt and wonder, "can we trust God?" In this story the question is turned the other way, "can God trust us?" I love that God suggested a celebration out of their faithfulness. The faithfulness of these two faithful servants bought them into a great intimacy with the master. It is as if the master is saying, "I am proud of you, I trusted you and you proved faithful, I want to celebrate with you."

There was no celebration offered to the servant who only received one bag of gold. He said of the master, "I knew that you are a hard man" (Matthew 25:24). The words, "I knew" indicate prior experience and knowledge. In all likelihood this is not the first time this servant has had to give an account. God looks to partner in mission and ministry with those who are faithful, those He can trust.

Ministry Birthed Out of Intimacy
Jesus was relational, not only with the Father, but with those He called to follow Him. We see this when He "went up on a mountainside and called to Him those He wanted, and they came to Him. He appointed twelve that they might be with Him and that He might send them out to preach and to have authority to drive out demons" (see Mark 3:13-15). He hung out with them. He trained them. He gave them authority. And He commissioned them to do the things He did.

One word of caution in our partnering with God: As important as serving God is, it is easy to get into a doing and a performing mode. We can get into doing and serving so much that we forget our effectiveness in doing flows out of the intimacy of being with God. In serving outside of what He has called us to, we will miss the intimacy of hearing.

Judas was a traitor, but of the eleven disciples, three were closer to Jesus than the rest, Peter, James, and John. Out of those three, John was closer than the others. Jesus closeness with John is not kept secret in the Bible, as John is called the "beloved disciple" (see John 21:20). Did Jesus play favorites? Why were the three closer to Him than the other eight? Why was one closer to Jesus than all the rest? The answers are a bit speculative, but it is more than gifts, personality traits, loyalty and obedience. I believe Peter, James and John were closer because they wanted to be. These three show through attitudes and behaviors that they loved being with Him, learning from Him and going wherever He went. It is not surprising that Peter, James, and John went on to be key leaders in the early Church. James was the first apostle martyred in the early Church.

If we were asked, are we as close to Jesus right now as we could be, most of us would answer "no." But truthfully, most of us are as close to Jesus as we want to be. Our hunger to be with Him at even inconvenient times is an indicator. Some of us as believers are not as close and intimate with Jesus because we are so caught up in our schedules and busyness which gives us a false sense of importance. When this happens Jesus gets the leftovers of our time and energy.

Assignments Through Open and Closed Doors
Some years ago, I pastored a church in Escondido, California. After serving this church for eight years I rather unexpectedly felt released from the assignment and knew that God was calling me to another ministry. I was so sure of God's nudge to a new ministry, I resigned not knowing where the Lord might lead. In my mind I had thought of one other church, but they had a pastor, so that did not seem likely. In the next weeks, a series of unforeseen circumstances developed, and the pastor of the church, that I had thought of fondly toward potential ministry suddenly, resigned. Their leadership team called me for an interview. This looked like a sure open door.

I went for a very intimidating interview and very shortly after the interview they called me and told me that I was not their guy! I was quite sure they had made a mistake. Mark Batterson said, "You can't pray for open doors without accepting closed doors. After all, one usually leads to the other. In a sense, the closed door equates to 'released from' and the open-door equals, 'called to'" (102). That is great advice that I wish would have known then.

The next six weeks were long and noticeably quiet with no open doors. Until I received a call to come interview at a church in Phoenix. I did not want to go. The opportunity sounded more like a ministry suicide mission. The venerated pastor was retiring and the leadership team of seven was comprised of five of the pastor's adult children. There was not an audible voice, or a whisper but God was clearly speaking through open and closed doors and the circumstances. I moved our family to Phoenix trusting God with fear and trembling as it was the only door that opened. Once the decision was made and I knew God had spoken through the circumstances I had a deep sense of peace. Looking back, thank God for the closed door and the open one. Those years in Phoenix were so fruitful and I learned so much.

Many times, God's plan unfolds gradually. He speaks in preparation to help us get ready. He speaks to help us be aware of timing and calls us to be watchful of opportunities. God longs to reveal opportunities, partnerships, and challenges to stretch us, surprise us and keep us walking in dependency on the wisdom and guidance of the Holy Spirit. While we serve Him through what He has spoken, impressed, and nudged we are experiencing the fellowship of ministry with Him. As He said to Joshua, "Do not be afraid: do not be discouraged, for the Lord God will be with you wherever you go" (Joshua 1:9) He is also saying to us.

Points to Ponder
What do you think about the statement: You are as close to God right now as you really want to be? What steps can you take this

week to go deeper in your relationship with the Lord and make sure you are not only hearing God but listening to Him?

Put yourself in Ananias' shoes, how would you have fared in that situation?

Focus for Prayer: *Father help me to be prepared for any future partnership with You whether they are big challenges or small behind the scenes acts of kindness. Most of all help me to not be so consumed with serving that I forget intimacy with you is most important.*

Chapter 6 – Discovering Guidance

Hearing His Voice

One evening in a home group, Cathy mentioned she had misplaced her keys. Cathy's key fob to her vehicle had been missing for about three weeks. One of the members of the group suggested, "you should pray about it, we should always pray about little things." The group didn't pray and Cathy didn't think more of the comment until one morning as she is about ready to crawl out of bed, she hears, the words spoken in the home group, "we should pray about little things." Cathy thought, "Okay God, where are my keys? Would you help me find them?" Cathy felt an immediate impression, "Check the bottom of the closet." The impression was strong enough that Cathy went and got a flashlight and got down on the floor amidst the shoes and at the back of the closet, there were her keys. Cathy laughed and rejoiced. God had helped her to find her keys.

A few weeks later Cathy had a similar experience. Her daughter had given her a pair of earrings, so the earrings were a very meaningful gift. Cathy, a teacher in the middle school, was in charge of changing the lettering on the school marquee. Upon coming in from the cold Wyoming winter day, Cathy realized that one of the earrings was missing. The brushed bronze finish on the earring was very much the color of the dead grass so Cathy searched all of the grass area but could not find the earring. That evening snow came. When it snows in Wyoming the snow can cover the ground for months. The maintenance crew always cleared space around the marquee so Cathy could change the lettering. Piling the fresh snow up on the side. Each time out there she looked for the earring. Some weeks later after the snow had melted, she decided to widen her search a bit and to search all of the grass, to no avail. Near the sign where she had searched a number of times, she remembers finding the key fob and the words, "pray about little things." Cathy again prayed "Lord help me find the earring." Immediately she felt impressed to look down, and right by her foot was the lost earring. Cathy now believes that God cares about little things that matter to us.

People who experience intimacy with God are dependent on Him for guidance. Discovering and receiving guidance from God is so much easier when we have learned and experienced the voice of God through intimacy with Him. Who would not want to depend on the One Who constantly sees the whole picture? If a needlepoint hoop was an illustration of the providence and wisdom of God, in the underneath view the threads go every which way, making no sense. When the pattern is seen from the top view of the hoop, the beauty of the needlepoint can be understood. God has the top view of our lives; we see the underside.

While we wait on God for direction and guidance, there is always something of Himself that He wants to show us and teach us, whether it be His character, His purpose, or His heart. People who value intimacy through hearing His voice do not pass up an opportunity to learn more about our God and live in dependency on Him.

David's Example of Seeking Guidance
David, a man after God's own heart, often inquired of the Lord. 1 Samuel 23:1-13 provides a great example of this, "When David was told, 'Look, the Philistines are fighting against Keilah and are looting the threshing floors,' he inquired of the Lord, saying, 'Shall I go and attack these Philistines?' The Lord answered him, 'Go, attack the Philistines and save Keilah'" (1 Samuel 23:1-2).

Some of David's men were fearful, so David in humility wanted to make sure he had heard God correctly, so again he inquired of the Lord. The answer came back a second time "yes go" (see 1 Samuel

23:4). One of the first rules of hearing from God is to assume that we could possibly be wrong. God does not seem to be impatient with David in asking for confirmation. Note, David did not keep asking and asking like we do when we do not want to do something. He asked the second time and then obeyed. It is a part of intimacy with God to honor Him with the attitude "God you are so important to me, I want to make sure I am getting this right."

A very similar story is found in 2 Samuel 5:17-25. The Philistines were on the attack again and David inquired of the Lord. Again, God gives the instruction, "Go, for I will surely deliver the Philistines into your hands" (see 2 Samuel 5:19). Later in that same chapter the Philistines were in attack mode again. Again, David inquired of the Lord. This situation must have looked much the same to David; but this time, God gave David a different strategy. God said, "Do not go straight up, but circle around behind them" (2 Samuel 5:23).

What can we learn from these stories? Intimacy relies on God for every situation, no matter how similar they may look. David did not assume that just because He had an anointing on his life that His victories were automatic. Inquiring of the Lord was David's consistent pattern in his relationship with God during the seasons in his life when he walked in intimacy with God. There were other seasons when David failed to inquire of the Lord as he had allowed his mind, eyes, and heart to be directed someplace other than God.

It is important to be directed by the Lord in every situation. Excellent devotional writer, Chris Tiegreen, adds:

> "We need specific guidance from God in every situation. Sure, there are times when we can count on wisdom He has already given, but we can't learn precepts and call that a relationship. The strategy He gave us yesterday may not apply today because the battles of life keep changing. We have to learn how to hear His voice and follow His lead. The Kingdom is given to those who listen carefully to the King (26).

People living in dependency on the Lord know not only that they need to hear, but that they can hear the voice of the Lord. God is faithful to give guidance to each incident.

Seeking Guidance Outside of Intimacy
David's predecessor Saul failed to develop intimacy with God and failed to seek the Lord through inquiring of Him. David walked in humility and intimacy while Saul walked in egotism. 1 Chronicles 10:13 provides a definitive testimony regarding Saul's life: "Saul died because he was unfaithful to the Lord; he did not keep the word of the Lord and even consulted a medium for guidance, and did not inquire of the Lord..." Charles Hummel in his must read booklet *The Tyranny of the Urgent* wrote: "But the root of all sin is self-sufficiency—independence from the rule of God. When we fail to wait prayerfully for God's guidance and strength, we are saying with our actions, if not with our words, that we do not need Him" (Goodread.com). Thinking we do not need to inquire of the Lord in each and every situation is prideful and arrogant.

Confirmation of the others in the Body of Christ is good, but many of us run here and there asking friends what they think should be done. There is no harm in gathering reliable information, but all the while the Lord is desiring to lead us, guide us, and speak wisdom to us. Saul neither sought the Lord or godly counsel consequently he displeased the Lord.

James 1:5 says, "If any of you lacks wisdom, you should ask God, Who gives generously to all without finding fault, and it will be given to you." I have always found this verse a bit humorous, "If any of you lack wisdom" is such an understated statement. It is not of matter of "if," because we all lack wisdom, it is a matter of "when." This verse speaks of the safe place God gives us in asking, He gives wisdom to us "generously." It is as if He is saying, "I am so glad you asked, because I am most glad to answer your need for wisdom." One reason most of us do not receive wisdom from the Lord is that we are a culture of wanting speedy answers. We are a snap decision, "strike while the iron is hot" society. Wisdom does not come with the snap of a finger but in waiting on the Lord for guidance.

Guidance - The Fruit of Intimacy with God
It is the nature of God to provide guidance and in the process reveal more of Himself to us. It makes no sense with our limited vision, perspective and information that we "go it alone," and do not avail ourselves to the guidance of God. In 1896 F. B. Meyer wrote *The Secret of Guidance,* since reprinted it is still one of the best books on the subject of guidance. Meyer says, "It seems a thousand pities that you should live a beggar's life when such wealth and power are yours; but if you persist in doing so, your folly and blindness do not alter the fact that the fulness of God is yours in Christ" (27). Through Christ all of the riches of wisdom are ours. There is so much more that we fail to avail ourselves to. We do not understand all that can be withdrawn from our heavenly account. Our inheritance is revealed in the intimacy of our relations with God.

God gives us some wonderful promises around hearing and guidance. As we seek His guidance consider these verses:
> Psalm 32:8 "I will instruct you and teach you in the way you should go; I will counsel you with my loving eye on you."

> Isaiah 30:21 "Whether you turn to the right or to the left, your ears will hear a voice behind you, saying, 'This is the way; walk in it.'"

> Isaiah 58:11 "The Lord will guide you always; He will satisfy your needs in a sun-scorched land and will strengthen your frame. You will be like a well-watered garden, like a spring whose waters never fail.

We live in a noisy world with all kinds of distractions. Some of these distractions are internal and external voices that seek to get our focus off God and onto ourselves, a sure recipe for spiritual disaster. Priscilla Shirer gives great advice for discerning these

voices when she writes:
> "When the enemy speaks to you, when your ego speaks to you, those voices will distort the character and Word of God. Anything that doesn't reflect the character of God or require you to more clearly see and experience Him is not a message from Him. Because this is His chief aim. He alone is our prize" (109).

We should frequently pray, "Lord quiet every voice in my head and heart but Your voice." May the Lord give us the ears to hear His voice and the eyes to see His heart.

Guidance Of Protection

I'll never forget the recent morning as I was pulling off the exit ramp on the freeway, that I heard, "Get ready for speed bumps." God's warning was not about driving tips, He was giving me warning that I was ready to enter a bumpy patch. The caution from God had barely ended when my phone pinged with the notice of an email. It was one of those terse emails one would rather not receive. That email was the first of several events over a ten-day period that were rather bumpy. I was so thankful to the Lord through that time, as His five words "get ready for speed bumps" aptly spoken, sustained me.

Psalm 91 speaks of God's protection. "He will call on me, and I will answer him; I will be with him in trouble" (Psalm 91:15). God shields, warns, and protects. He warned Joseph in a dream to take Jesus to Egypt for safety and there is story after story in the Bible of God leading people out of harm's way and offering His protection. He is still speaking words of guidance and protection. Brother Yun, referred to as the "Heavenly Man" in China in his book *Living Water* writes regarding God's miraculous guidance and protection for the underground church in China:

> On numerous occasions, preachers in China have traveled to a remote mountainous area to visit a group of believers. Although nobody is told that they are coming, when the preachers arrive they often find the believers already

gathered together and expecting them, sometimes even in the middle of the night! When asked how they knew the preachers were coming at that time, they reply, "The Lord told us to get ready because you were coming at this time." In other places, the house churches had problems when undercover agents came along to spy on the believers and see if they could gather information that might be used against them later. The Christians prayed and asked God what they should do. The Lord told them to stop announcing the place and time of their meetings and instead just trust that the Holy Spirit would reveal the details to each person He wanted to come to the meeting. On the day of the next meeting, nobody except the leader knew where the church service would be held, or at what time, but one by one believers began to turn up, all having been told where to go while they were praying earlier that morning. This method is one way of making sure that only those people the Lord wants to fellowship together actually do so (131-132).

Such is God's love for us and for all of the Body of Christ who seek Him and long for His protection, help and direction in our lives.

When We Are Called to Wait

God not only brings guidance and protection; His timing is perfect. Few things are as aggravating to us as a waiting room. We have an appointment, but we find ourselves stuck reading outdated and worn out magazines. We frequently find ourselves in waiting rooms in our lives. Things we have prayed about and in faith expected, are not happening, at least at the pace we were anticipating. Herein lies a great danger, the human heart is deceitful enough to think this waiting is a sign to take things into our own hands and move ahead.

We fail to understand that the process and the waiting are as important as the result of the journey. There are character traits of God's we cannot know outside of waiting. There are character flaws regarding us we cannot know outside of the disappointment of waiting. God values heart preparation. He knows to be placed in a situation before we have been seasoned and properly prepared will bring sure failure. He loves us too much to release us in certain circumstances or situations before we are ready. Even the Son of God, Jesus, had thirty years of preparation and only three years of ministry.

Psalm 27:14 says, "Wait for the Lord; be strong and take heart and wait for the Lord." There is joy in the waiting when we understand that it is not always about preparation, sometimes it is about timing. When our daughter was born it seemed like she would never come. Four weeks before the due date, the doctor told my wife and me, "we may have miscalculated the due date. Stay close to home, this baby could come at any time." We were elated and got busy putting finishing touches on the nursery thinking "the baby could come at any time." Elated until the four weeks later when the original due date passed. Hearing the doctor's encouragement, "just be patient" did not seem helpful. Now past the original due date, my prayers are turning a little edgy, even angry. I was praying the "God, don't you know what is going on here?" kind of prayers, we have all prayed. (Please tell me I am not the only one).

The lesson, and the baby girl, came two weeks' later, but in God's plan that was right on time. I'll never forget the doctor saying, "her lungs are just barely developed, good thing she wasn't born earlier." Oh, thank you Lord for not answering my angry prayer! Your timing is perfect.

Finding Guidance
So how do I find guidance for my life? Guidance is not a proverbial needle in a haystack, it is an outflow of knowing Him and being constantly available to Him. Guidance is the fruit of intimacy. Intimacy takes time, we want a tree when God gives us an acorn and tells us to plant it. We have grown accustomed to the speed of light and microwaves, but often God is moving at the speed of a seed.

I recently traveled with our 7-year-old granddaughter. We were not 15 minutes up the freeway before the words, "how much longer" followed by many, many, many "are we there yet?" questions were asked. Her definition of time is quite different than mine as her personal time reference is only seven years and mine, double digitally much longer. I wish I could say I was totally serene with her questions. As we wait for guidance, know it will come but "do not forget this one thing, dear friends: With the Lord a day is like a thousand years, and a thousand years are like a day" (2 Peter 3:8). As we find ourselves waiting on God and answers we should remember that His sense of time is way different than ours.

Guidance comes easier for individuals who spend time in God's Word. The Scriptures contain all the principles of wisdom and direction. The Scripture is not a substitute for asking the Guide, the Holy Spirit, for instructions. We can do the right thing, but if we do the right thing with the wrong timing, we will experience the wrong result. We must always ask Him for His timing. And as we ask, know that what He speaks will never lead us contrary to what the Scripture says.

Points to Ponder
Take a fresh look at Proverbs 3:5-6 and Psalm 25:4-5. What do these passages say to you about the Lord's guidance in your life?

Here are two thoughts worth processing:
- When you get your eyes on the circumstances God's strength may seem to be diminished.
- The monotony of day by day living lulls us into forgetting how powerful God can be.

Focus for Prayer: *Father teach me new and fresh that You have my best interest at heart. Forgive me for the times I take things into my own hands, instead of trusting Your perfect timing.*

Chapter 7 – Familiarity with the Voice of the Lord

Hearing His Voice

While God speaks to us in our thoughts, we do not always distinguish them from our own thoughts, Scott and Stephanie share their experience. Stephanie writes:

"My sisters, cousins and my family had all gathered at my parents' house one Saturday. The adults were inside, and the kids were outside. My dad came in the front door holding our 3-year-old middle child who had blood running down her leg. She had been swinging when she went crooked and caught her leg on a bolt. The bolt snagged her skin and caused a large section to peel off and roll up inside itself. We wrapped it in a clean towel and Scott and I took her to an Urgent Care facility nearby. After about a dozen tiny numbing shots and 13 stitches, the doctor on call (who had done an extensive plastic surgery rotation previously) said with a smile 'well, I think we got all of her back in there.'"

"As we were driving home, I was sitting in the back with Amelia who was looking at her new book with buttons that made sounds and I was pondering Psalm 91, specifically verse 11-12.

For He shall give His angels charge over you,
To keep you in all your ways.
In their hands they shall bear you up,
Lest you dash your foot against a stone.

I had just silently asked God 'Is it even possible to live a Psalm 91 life in today's world.' The moment that silent prayer was sent to God's ears, Scott, from the seat in front of me said emphatically 'I knew I should have done something about that bolt!' I froze staring at the back of his head. 'What?' I asked surprised. 'Every time I walked by that swing set my eyes went to that bolt and I thought I should do something to fix it.' Scott had seen that swing set for 10 years but never before had that thought...The answer was 'Yes'" We can live in a Psalm 91 world when we learn to recognize God's voice, His leading, His instructions."

"Why didn't angels stop her from hurting her leg. I don't know. But I do know God is watching over us at all times and is speaking to us to help us live the life He wants us to live. We need to learn to distinguish His voice from our own."

When my wife calls me on the phone, she has no need to announce herself or tell me her name, because we are intimate and close. Her tones, cadence and voice inflections are all familiar. When a telephone rings the people in the room can see by the expression on the face of the person who answers the degree of familiarity, whether a dear friend, an acquaintance, or a stranger with a spam call. A baby is familiar with his/her mother's voice and even the music mom likes before being born. Medical science discovered that a baby in the womb knows the mother's voice after 25 weeks and the Father's voice after 32 weeks into the pregnancy (Healthline.com). Jesus declared that His sheep follow Him because they know His voice, (see John 10:4-5).

Blackaby and King said, "Right now God is working all around you and in your life. One of the greatest tragedies among God's people is that, while they have a deep longing to experience God, they are experiencing God day after day but do not know how to recognize Him" (15). The key to familiarity is time, specifically the amount of time we spend fellowshipping with and worshipping the Lord. The more time we spend with a friend the more we know how that friend thinks, speaks and acts. The same is true in the time we spend with our Lord. God desires us to be very familiar with His voice.

We should practice hearing God's voice; it is a learning process. There are times I thought I heard from God only to find out later I had missed or misconstrued what I thought I had heard. There have been other times that God spoke, and I missed hearing and several times I was disobedient to what I heard. When I was first learning to hear God's voice, I was in a McDonalds restaurant when God communicated a specific message to give to a man sitting several tables away from me in the dining room. I was full of excuses for not taking the risk of sharing with the man what I had heard. Perhaps there are situations where we move on and forget about it, but these 30 years later I know without a doubt God spoke a message to deliver and I did not do it. I can picture the man to this day. God is patient with us, especially when He knows we want to get it right. He wants to be heard even more than we want to hear Him. Time and spiritual maturity help us to develop intimacy with God and practicing hearing makes us familiar with His voice.

God helps us develop familiarity with His voice. We see this with the boy Samuel. God spoke to Samuel four times in a row until young Samuel understood it was the voice of the Lord. Samuel had mistakenly thought the priest Eli who was sleeping in the next room was calling to him. God was patient with him as he developed his hearing. There is no indication in the Bible record that Samuel confused God's voice again. He knows each of us so well that He knows how to speak in a way that we can hear and understand.

The Frequency of God Speaking
The frequency of God speaking may vary from person to person, but the most important thing about the frequency of God speaking is obedience. Dallas Willard says, "Perhaps we do not hear the voice because we do not expect to hear it. Then again, perhaps we do not expect it because we know that we fully intend to run our lives on our own and have never seriously considered any-

thing else" (93). In some cases when God does not tell us what we were hoping or wanting to hear, we just stop listening. It is easy to draw attention away from our disobedience by excusing ourselves with the unbelief that "God just does not speak."

There is a definite correlation between our hearing and our obedience to the Spirit and the Word. The word *obedient* comes from the Latin word *audire*, which means listening or to pay attention (www.latin-dictionary.net). This correlation is also found in the Greek language. The word for "I hear" is akouō, the same root word as "I obey," hupakouō. The proof of our hearing is listening and obedience to what He says. Little creates closeness and oneness with God like doing what He says to do. This intimacy is spoken of in Psalm 25:14 in the *Amplified Bible Classic Edition*: "The secret [of the sweet, satisfying companionship] of the Lord have they who fear (revere and worship) Him, and He will show them His covenant and reveal to them its [deep, inner] meaning." A spiritual life requires discipline because we need to learn to listen to God, who constantly speaks even though we sometime fail to hear. When we learn to listen, our lives become obedient lives. Our actions demonstrate whether or not we listen.

Some people say that God never speaks to them. In almost every case there has been a breach in obedience. Why should God speak a fresh word to us when we have refused to obey the last word He spoke? When we make the decision to follow God's directions, knowing He has our best interest at heart, we will have little trouble developing familiarity to His voice. Obedience to the voice of the Spirit is important to experiencing His blessing and seeing His anointing and power flowing through us.

Discerning His Voice
There are many voices all around us clamoring for our attention, including our own. The more familiar I am with the Lord's voice the easier it will be to discern the voices of the world, the flesh, and the devil. It can be difficult to discern the voice of the accuser

because he loves to sound religious and scriptural and tries to get us to believe a half-truth laced with a lie. Francis Frangipane is really helpful when he says: "You will recognize the voice of the enemy for it never offers hope or extends grace for repentance. It as acts as though it is the voice of God and we are guilty of the 'unpardonable sin'" (98). The voice of God always provides a way out and a way through; always leading us to victory, not defeat. The enemy loves to seek to pile on guilt feelings long after God has forgiven our sin.

Familiarity with a voice helps us discern who is speaking. An illustration of familiarity comes from banking industry. Tellers are taught to spot counterfeit bills by spending plenty of time counting genuinely real bills. The more accustomed the teller is to the real bills the easier time she/he will have identifying the fake. The same principle is true as it relates to the voice of God. The more time we spend listening the more familiar we become with the voice that speaks. My mother and father have been in heaven for many years now, but I can still hear the sounds of their voices in my mind.

Guidelines To Hearing

There are a few helpful guidelines in hearing. We should ask, "does what we are hearing help us keep our eyes on Jesus?" When our focus is solely on Jesus the battle vanishes almost immediately. Does what we are hearing cause us to feel a sense of hopeless? If it does, it is not the voice of the Lord. Bill Johnson says, "Any area of our lives for which we have no hope is under the influence of a lie" (168). Ask, does what we have heard bring a sense of peace or a sense of conflict? The voice of the Lord is gentle and full of peace. If the voice leaves us deeply troubled inside, we should be suspect of the source of what we have heard. Isaiah 26:3 (CEV) says, "The Lord gives perfect peace to those whose faith is firm." The other important question to ask is, does what we are hearing bring us into a deeper dependency on the Lord? The voice of the Lord always moves us away from self-dependency toward intimacy and reliance on Him.

In this process we should be patient with ourselves, knowing that God is patient with us as we learn. Do not worry that you do not hear like Ezekiel, Daniel or John the "Beloved Disciple." When we offer God the heart to hear Him, He will take care of the mechanisms of our hearing to help us gain familiarity with His voice. Do not worry, God wants to be heard.

Points to Ponder

What steps can you take to offer your heart to God in order to better hear Him?

Why is intimacy with God so important in becoming familiar with His voice? I say to the Lord frequently that I love the sound of His voice and that I long to hear it.

If we have not heard God speak in a long time, we should ask ourselves, "Did I obey the last thing God said?" Perhaps God is waiting for us to do what He has already said.

Focus for Prayer: *Lord I want to make my heart and my ears open to hear Your voice. Help me to be so familiar with You and Your ways that when You speak, I can quickly obey because I know it is You and I know that You have my best interest at heart.*

Chapter 8 – Listening Beyond Hearing

Hearing His Voice

A pastor in the underground church in Laos shared, "by whisper with confirmation of the Bible I am confident the Lord calls me to do three things: First, reach out to people in the village to share gospel and teach the Bible for new church planting and to develop new church leaders in Laos especially in the Luang Prabang area. Second to start youth groups in the city helping students to grow in their faith that they can learn to share the gospel on their college campuses. Third, God willing we will start a Bible training center in Luang Prabang." This pastor's great faith is being used by God in a powerful way.

During my days in school I heard my share of the words, "pay attention!" It was my teacher's way of asking if I was listening. While dating my wife, Marlyce, listening was a big subject. She not only wanted to be heard, she wanted to feel listened to. I made a promise to be a good listener. I had no idea how much work I needed to put into this skill to keep that promise. As a man when I heard what she was saying, I wanted to fix it for her by utilizing my great masculine "fix it" skills. It took a while to understand she did not want me to fix anything, she just wanted to be heard. She wanted me to listen to her.

This challenge to listen is nothing new. My mother used to say to me as a teenager "I think that went in one ear and right out the other." She would ask "Are you hearing me? I know you hear, but are you hearing me?" Mom was asking "if I was listening?"

Listening is an important component of every relationship. Listening is one of the ways the other person feels valued and loved. Many of us have work to do in the area of listening. For the other person to feel listened to, our eyes and ears need to work in concert. If we are not making eye contact, the other person can tell we are hearing, but not really listening. To fully listen, we must pay attention.

Just Text Me
We are losing much relational closeness with one another through the use of our cell phones. Many people no longer answer their phones or pick up voice mails. "Just text me, it is so much easier," we say. Yes is easier, but we cannot hear the sound of each other's voice. Without the voice there is a loss of intimacy. We receive the information in the text message, but we do not get the benefit of hearing the persons voice and the tones of the heart.

Even when we do take the call, our phones allow us to multi-task. Unfortunately, we can get on a cell phone and wander around doing other tasks while we are talking —but this begs the question as to whether we are actually really listening and truly hearing what the other person says. Most of the time we listen to music or books online when we are doing other things—driving or working. Sometimes it all becomes just noise and we are not really listening.

Whoever Has Ears
We have ears so we have the capacity to hear, but just because we have the capacity to hear does not mean that we have acuity and passion to hear. The Bible records the expression, "whoever has ears let them hear" fourteen times; six times in the Gospels and then eight times in the book of Revelation. Henri Nouwen in his book *Spiritual Direction* says, "Developing 'ears to hear' God takes time. We all have strong resistances to listening. We find it very hard to create empty spaces in our lives and to give up our occupations and preoccupations even for a little while" (18). We often are thinking of what we are going to say before the other person is done speaking. Lacking listening skills, we tend to craft our

next sentences instead of truly listening. Many times in receiving directions or an address or more importantly a story from a grandparent later we wish we would have listened more carefully. Boredom or preoccupation keep us from truly listening.

When the Bible uses the phrase, "let the one who has ears hear what the Spirit says," it is saying, do more than hear, let it go deep into your heart. The study of anatomy teaches us there is an outer ear, a middle ear, and an inner ear. Each of these has a specific and intricate function in getting the sound waves to the brain where what is heard is interpreted. When my Mom used the expression "in one ear and out the other" she was saying "you are not allowing what I've said to go into your inner ear." Mark Batterson says, "When Jesus said, 'Whoever has ears, let them hear, I think it's an exhortation to listen not once but twice. It's in that gap between the first hearing and second hearing were we discern the prompting of the Holy Spirit" (41) The Lord is telling us to listen deeply, take in deep into our heart.

Several years ago, I had the privilege of attending a Japanese Taiko drum concert. Having never been to a drum concert before certain things surprised me. The synchronicity and precision of the drummers was beautiful to watch. The drums created loud sounds and deep vibrations which could not only be heard but felt from head to toe. The thing that shocked me most about the concert is that over half of the audience was comprised of deaf individuals who could not hear the sounds but could enjoy the movement and feel the vibrations.

In a conversation about the challenges with physical hearing, our dear friend Chris, a Recipient Service Market Specialist for a major hearing implant company made an astute observation about spiritual hearing. Chris said, "We are all deaf in a sense because we don't recognize it or want to recognize that we don't hear. It doesn't fit our lifestyle or the path we are on or our hearts are not open to hearing." Hearing the voice of the Lord is enhanced by earnestly wanting to hear and taking what He says deep into our hearts.

Hearing Versus Listening

We sometimes use the terms hearing and listening interchangeably, but they are distinctively different. Hearing is more of a physiological function; listening is a choice as to what we let into our inner ear and heart. You cannot help what you hear, but you can choose what you listen to. There are certain noises that are familiar and when we hear that noise, we then tune our ears to listen, because we do not want to miss what is to come. We listen for someone we expect to hear. My ears are tuned to the sound of the garage door going up at about 5:10 each afternoon. The sound alerts my hearing which causes me to listen for the car door to close, my wife's footsteps, and her first words after her long day at work. I am anxious to catch up and listen regarding her day.

We hear a lot that we pay no attention to. There is noise all around which we seldom notice. There are times we hear gossip that we wish we had not heard, but just because we heard it, does not mean we have to listen to it. There are many sounds we should not let get into our inner ear.

I have noticed as I am aging that my hearing is not quite as keen and yet my ears seem to be getting larger. I was relieved to know that our ears do not grow larger, the cartilage in our ears relaxes making them appear larger. Bigger ears seem to play no part in hearing better, because for most of us the problem is not that we are hard of hearing, we are simply hard of listening.

As we mature in our walk with the Lord, we should tune our ears to hear, so that when He speaks, we can carefully listen. We know the sound of His voice will bring something valuable to listen to. A message of importance worth taking deep into our hearts. We listen to who we care about and we listen to what is important to us. As your intimacy with Abba Father grows so will your hearing and listening.

Making Space

Listening involves processing what we have heard, thinking about it, and taking what has been said to heart. Listening usually requires a response beyond the nod of the head. True listening means to make some space for another person. We desperately need to create some space in our lives to listen to God. A spiritual life requires discipline because we need to learn to listen to God, who constantly speaks even though we seldom hear. When we learn to listen, our lives become obedient and fruitful.

There is much noise and many voices calling out for our attention. Our world is full of media distractions, job worries and financial pressures. To make space means I still all of the voices, including my own, that I might truly listen to what is important. We need to still the voice of what we think others might be thinking of us. (Usually they are not, it is us imagining they are). We need to quiet the voices of past failures which become a filter through which we hear incorrectly or not at all. We definitely need to silence the voice that says, "We are not good enough." These self-doubt voices can cause a hearing deficit to the voice of the God Who calls us into intimacy and says, to each of us "I love you and value you."

Whatever the voice, what we consistently listen to tells us what our priorities are and who or what is important in our lives. Francis Frangipane in *Spiritual Discernment and the Mind of Christ* says:
> We must learn how to pause before we speak - give ourselves a moment to enter the secret place of God's presence and then listen to what Jesus has to say….in listening, we create the opportunity to hear the Lord's voice; postured before Him we can receive answers, wisdom and insights that we otherwise would not discern (25).

The God of the universe is looking for people who will make the space to listen to what He wants to say, to listen to His kind whisper of intimacy. What a privilege is ours!

God is not like the parents who constantly scream at their children. God will speak in a way to get our attention and to help us hear; He does not typically yell. "God will speak to the heart of those who prepare themselves to hear; and conversely; those who do not prepare themselves will hear nothing even though the Word of God is falling upon their outer ears every Sunday" (A.W. Tozer, 27-28). When we prepare ourselves and expect ourselves to hear from God the likelihood of hearing increases exponentially. Henri Nouwen says, "Listening is the core attitude of the person who is open to God's living and creative word" (88).

Marks of a Genuine Listener
We have all had the experience at a conference or event where there are many people that the person we were talking to was looking passed our eyes over our shoulder to see if there is someone else he/she wants to talk to. They were hearing you but not really listening. We felt devalued like they would talk to us until someone more interesting comes along. A good listener is attentive to what is being said. Eye contact and body language indicates engagement in the conversation. Arms crossed or fidgeting always communicates that we are not listening. Someone interested in what we are saying repeats back what they have heard, or they ask clarifying questions. Good listeners do not multitask. It is hard to listen to another person when we are checking our phone for emails or messages.

A genuine listener does not complete the other persons sentences with the unspoken attitude "I am going to help you tell me this story because it is taking you too long." A good listener stays in a learning process and carries the attitude, "If I listen, I might learn something." We show impatience by using clichés, such as, "I know just how you feel." The truth is, we might have an idea and a sense of empathy, but none of us truly knows how the other feels.

These are social blunders we sometimes make in our conversations with other people. We make some of these same mistakes with God in that in our self-talk and negativity we are interrupting Him and talking over the top of His voice. There are things He wants to say but the unbelief in our hearts is talking so loudly we miss the message of freedom and blessing He is wanting us to hear. Just as everyone wants to be understood, God wants us to understand not only His heart but what He is communicating to us.

Selective Hearing

Many read the Scriptures using, what I like to call, the "dip and skip method." When we read using this method, we "dip" into the parts we like, such as the promises and good stories but "skip" the parts we are less comfortable with. It is easy to adopt this same method in our listening to God. "If we don't listen to everything God has to say, we eventually won't hear anything He has to say" (Batterson 56-57). Remember, God's primary purpose in speaking is intimacy. He invites us to relationship, partnership, and fellowship. He calls us to come to Him as He has our best interest at heart. In speaking to us He shows us the way. Isaiah 30:21 says, "Whether you turn to the right or to the left, your ears will hear a voice behind you, saying, 'This is the way; walk in it.'" When we listen to the voices of our own opinions, we limit God's voice. As a result, the outcomes for our lives are less than His best.

It is easier to listen when we are in an invigorating conversation and exchange with a dear friend, than when one or the other of us does all of the talking. Conversation with a friend is the setting described in Revelation 3:20. Often misused out of context, it is the voice of Jesus calling us into fellowship and conversation. "Behold, I stand at the door and knock. If anyone hears My voice and opens the door, I will come into him and dine with him, and he with Me" (Revelation 3:20 NKJV). It puts a whole new meaning on the verse when we understand the Lord is wooing us for conversation, for our questions, and to provide His answer to us.

When we determine to listen to God through both His Word and through the Spirit's voice we will live in confidence. We will experience the courage to live above fear. Proverbs 1:33 (TPT) says, "But the one who always listens to Me will live undisturbed in a heavenly peace. Free from fear, confident and courageous, you will rest unafraid and sheltered from the storms of life." Believers who listen will hear of the values of heaven and will understand how to apply those values here on earth. We will live in constant victory because we realize the value of our relationship with God. We prize intimacy with Him above all else.

∞∞∞

Points to Ponder
Do you agree that listening is wanting to hear?

What steps can you take to be a better listener to your loved ones? To the voice of God?

What does Ephesians 2:6 say about who you are in Christ?

Focus for Prayer: *Lord help me to be less preoccupied with the things of earth, things that hinder me from hearing Your precious voice and having deep intimacy with You. Help me to learn to value the things You value.*

Chapter 9 – Hearing Loss

Hearing His Voice

Gerry Bishop worked in the oil fields as an oil pumper. On a wintry day Gerry and her crew were driving on treacherously slick roads between Buffalo and Kaycee, Wyoming. Gerry doesn't remember sliding off the road or the accident, her first memories are in the Medical Center of Billings. The doctor met with Gerry's family just at the edge of the room and said, "In all likelihood Gerry will not walk again." Gerry heard a voice audible to her, "We'll see about that!" Gerry said, "the voice was so clear and definite that I did not doubt that God had spoken." Gerry left the hospital in a wheelchair unable to walk but the words she had heard rang in her ears. A friend, name Lou, taught Gerry to crawl, and for some months she crawled, still not forgetting the words, "We'll see about that." Today Gerry walks everywhere and uses her scroll saw as a ministry.

This last year I had the privilege of ministering to 45 brave pastors in the underground church in Laos. While I was ministering in Laos, I kept feeling like this must have been what the book of Acts felt like. It was wonderful! Because preaching the gospel in Laos is illegal, I had to trust the voice of the Holy Spirit to lead me and protect me. As a result, I experienced great boldness to witness for Jesus, especially to taxi and tuk-tuk (small motor bikes with open seating in the back) drivers. Upon communicating my desired destination, I asked the driver "how much?" and once we settled on the fare, we would be off. On the way to the destination, I asked the Holy Spirit how much He would want me to give to the driver in addition to the fare. I learned two things. First, the Holy Spirit loves to be really generous. Second, generosity opens the door to talking to people about Jesus. I had the opportunity to pray with or talk to every driver about Jesus except for one. On that occasion the Holy Spirit warned me that the driver was an informant and that I should not speak of Jesus.

I have often been asked if I ever felt in danger, and the answer is "yes, once." Because I had had such success in speaking to drivers about Jesus, I got a little too confident. One evening as I was leaving the street market, a driver asked me if I needed a ride. I replied that I did and gave the destination. He invited me to ride in the small truck cab with him. I was halfway in the truck when the Holy Spirit whispered, "No this is not a good idea!" But since I was halfway in the cab, I did not reverse my course and say to the driver, "no thanks." Now in the moving cab I immediately knew I had not obeyed the voice of the Holy Spirit. I felt this deep sense of darkness. The driver had no more than pulled away from the curb when he asked, "What do you want – Heroin? Cocaine? Opium? – I have it all – just tell me what you want!" I said with as much confidence as I could muster, "Absolutely not, I help people get delivered from those kinds of drugs, and Jesus can deliver you too!" Because I had not been careful with the Spirit's voice, there did not seem to be much anointing on my words. So, I immediately repented, seeking forgiveness for my carelessness and asked for safety. I knew it was only by the grace of God that I did not get beaten up and robbed. I was never so glad to see the small inn where I was staying.

I was seeking to serve the Lord, but my over confidence and carelessness gave me a hearing loss. Over confidence can cause you to miss or underestimate the Holy Spirit's whisper. After this dark ride, I was always conscious to ask the Lord to pick my drivers for me.

When We Trust in Our Own Strength
There is nothing better than serving the Lord and hearing His voice as we carry out His calling. But ironically, one of the great-

est hearing losses can come from serving the Lord when we are working for Him in our own strength. It is easy to get overconfident in our service or not taking time to inquire of Him regarding what He has called us to do. It is also easy to serve to the degree we get spiritually depleted and then keep going not understanding that our spiritual tank is empty. Empty because of the great lack of fellowship with the Lord and our spiritual hearing dries up. When we do not inquire of the Lord and take time to listen to Him it is easy to be doing what we do in our own power.

We limit our effectiveness in ministry because we are not taking time to hear His voice in determining the who, the what and the when of what the Father wants us to accomplish for and with Him. Jennie Allen in her compelling book *Get Out of Your Head*, writes, "Why is the simplest, best thing for our souls' long-term health so crazy difficult to do? I'll tell you: because real, connected, intimate time with Jesus is the very thing that grows our faith…To put it plainly: all hell is against us meeting with Jesus" (70). Many are attempting to do good things, but because we are not taking time to meet with Jesus and fellowship with God, we are doing many activities He never called us to do.

Sometimes our ministry involves good things, but God has not promised to give us strength for ministries and projects He has not called us to. In serving God with a project that God has not assigned to us, Dallas Willard poignantly asks, "Why should God speak to me? What am I doing in life that would make speaking to me a reasonable thing for Him to do…am I in business just for myself, trying to 'use a little God' to advance my projects?" (94). When there seems to be no fruit or blessing from our ministries, we must quiet ourselves before God and ask: "Is this truly an assignment that You gave or a self-assignment?" Remember Jesus did not do anything that the Father was not showing Him to do. John 5:19 says, "The Son can do nothing by Himself; He can do only what He sees His Father doing, because whatever the Father does the Son also does." Once we have confirmation in our spirit that it is His assignment for us, we should listen for His voice for next steps. If it is not an assignment that He has given, we must stop at once.

Loss Through Noise
We get so used to noise we hardly pay attention to sounds of traffic, jack hammers, heavy equipment, and loud music. Even call centers pump in grey noise to lessen the possibility of their customers hearing of other voices. Grey noise "complements the acoustics of the human ear, so that to a listener, it sounds as if every frequency is equally loud" (Techopedia). Noise experts define different frequency of sound by color, so there is pink, brown, white, and red noise. Many people are so consumed by noise they even use it to help them sleep. Some parents put a television in their children's rooms thinking the noise will help the child sleep better. There is noise all around us. We are so used to noise that extreme quiet can almost seem to unnerve us. When we drive deep in the mountains the thing we notice most is the quiet.

We can get so unknowingly addicted to noise that we are afraid of silence and yet it is through getting quiet and stilling other voices that we start to hear God's intimate whisper. Because God often whispers we miss Him in the noise and He typically will not compete with other noises to get our attention. It is when we quiet our hearts before Him, that we hear.

Praying From our Own Agenda
It is hard to hear God correctly when we are too emotionally involved in an issue. To put it another way it is hard to hear from God in an area where we have not submitted ourselves to His Lordship. Overly involved emotions become like white noise roaring away, God's voice fades. The answer to this issue is to keep our hearts and eyes firmly fixed on Jesus determining that nothing is more important than our intimacy with Him.

Ezekiel 14:4 is a verse that we should often ponder: "This is what the Sovereign Lord says: When any of the Israelites set up idols in their hearts and put a wicked stumbling block before their faces and then go to a prophet, I the Lord will answer them Myself in keeping with their great idolatry." In offering commentary on this verse Mark and Patti Virkler say, "If I pray about an item and the item is more prominent in my vision or my consciousness than my vision of the Lord, the answer that comes back will be from the item rather than from the Lord" (43).

We will always be dull of hearing if we have already determined in our minds what we want before even bringing it to the Lord. Areas where we should exercise great care in praying with an agenda is a major purchase (car or house), choosing a mate, or job change. There is a subtle idolatry in wanting what we want and wanting God to help us get it, instead of seeking what God wants for us. Whenever we want what God can do more than we want God for Himself, we will have skewed spiritual hearing. God speaks to people who have determined they want His purpose and plan above all else.

God wants to bless and favor us as His children, but we need in humility to trust Him for the timing of His blessing. That God will not give us more than we can handle is not only true in the area of temptation, it is also in the area of blessing. He will not bless us beyond our ability to steward the blessing. God will never furnish us the ammunition for arrogance.

Along with self-promotion comes the loss of being able to hear God's voice correctly. F.B. Meyer aptly says, "So long as there is some thought of personal advantage, some idea of acquiring the praise and commendation of men, some aim at self-aggrandizement, it will be simply impossible to find out God's purpose concerning us" (7). Pride is such a dangerous trap to fall into, it is dangerous because it always places self on the throne. It causes us to seek our own happiness instead of the deep fulfillment of joy flowing out of the presence of God. God is not interested in aiding us in anything that will take away from our anointing or the intimacy we share with Him.

Exhaustion
When we are exhausted or anxious it will be more difficult to hear Him clearly. When we are depleted of energy the noises inside our heads seem to become very active. When life is pressing in on us, it is easy to not only have hearing loss, but to improperly distinguish the voice of the Holy Spirit. Psalm 46:10, "Be still, and know that I am God" is always good advice during times of weariness. When you are exhausted it is not the best time to make life changing decisions.

We should not attempt to be a hero by forging through exhaustion, we should get some much-needed rest. Without rest we can get all turned in on ourselves and our troubles get magnified. We should ask the Lord to give us sleep, to stop the racing of our minds so that we can rest. We may ask God to protect us from dreams that He is not giving us, trusting that "in peace I will lie down and sleep, for You alone, Lord make me dwell in safety" (see Psalm 4:8).

After getting some rest, feed on the promises of God's Word. My Bible is well marked with these passages that offer me spiritual sustenance. Believe God for *rhema*, a freshly spoken word. As we feed on God's Word, we have the assurance that when He speaks, He will say nothing contrary to the Scripture.

Other Hindrances to Hearing
There are other things that can create spiritual hearing loss. First, people do not expect to hear so they are not listening even though God may be speaking. Second, some have hearing loss from their sense of unworthiness. This hearing loss causes them to think that anything they are hearing is just their wild and crazy imagination. Out of unworthiness comes negative self-talk. Mark Batterson says:

> ...you've been deafened by the negative self-talk that doesn't let God get a word in edgewise. Maybe you've listened to

the voice of criticism so long you can't believe anything else about yourself. If you don't silence those competing voices, they'll eventually deafen you (2).

In addition to negative self-talk, when we are preoccupied with schedules, things, and other people; we will be paying attention to those things instead of listening for the voice of God.

Not hearing from God clearly or at all because we go right through stop or yield signs He has given is dangerous. Some of us have drawn the conclusion that God is not speaking, but more often than not it is us having a hearing loss. Instead of drawing the conclusion that He is not speaking to us, we should determine that He does speak so we will do everything necessary to prepare to hear Him.

Points to Ponder
What do you think about the concept that God will not bless us beyond our ability to steward the blessing? Are there blessings you have received that you need to steward more completely?

Examine your heart as you read Ezekiel 14:4; ask the Lord to show you if there are areas you are placing in front of your relationship with Him.

About exhaustion or spiritual depletion: one little way of thinking has really helped me personally manage emotional "ups and downs". Most of us are not strangers to the emotional "ups and downs" of life. I agree with Charlie Brown "all I want is ups" but life does not work that way for Charlie and does not for us either. When I am in an emotional "up" period, it is easy to celebrate and think, "Wow, finally I am up!" I try to not allow myself to celebrate the 'up' excessively, but to save a little energy, by simply thinking, "I am up now but there will come a 'down.'" By thinking this way, I am not blindsided by the next trial, the next "down" time. What this does for me is it makes my "highs" a little lower and it makes my "lows" a little higher. Then when I am in a more depleted time, a low, I remember the "down" will not last, I will have an "up" again!

Prayer Focus: *Lord teach me to discern where I have hearing loss. I ask that You give me listening ears. Teach me to continually find rest in Your presence and carefully listen to Your nurturing whisper.*

Chapter 10 – Positioning Yourself to Hear

Hearing His Voice

John writes: *"Several years ago I had some circumstances in my life that seemed to be lose-lose. No matter what I did I could not win or break even. One day in the middle of the day I had to go to town for some reason, so I took my dirty work clothes off and got in the shower to clean up. I started talking to God about the situation in which I found myself.*

After I vented to my Heavenly Father for a while, I heard in my spirit a soft voice say, 'You are mad at me.' My reaction was to scoff and say, 'No I am not!' Then God seemed to speak in a more parental voice, 'Yes, yes you are.' That stopped me in my tracks and caused me to think. Then I had to respond to God with honesty and admit that I was not only mad at Him, but several other people also. As I was venting with honesty to God, I was hit with a thought that had to come from the Holy Spirit, because it came right out of the blue and had nothing to do with the road I was going down with God. The thought was straight out of a cartoon. It was, 'I have seen the enemy and it is me.' My anger at the lose-lose situation was affecting my attitudes and my attitudes were affecting my responses toward God and other people. I was making things worse instead of better. I was not trusting God with the situation. As soon as this hit me, feelings of sorrow and repentance washed over me like the water from the shower head. 'Oh my God, You are so right. I am my own worst enemy. Please forgive me for being so angry.' That was the best shower I have ever taken because when I was done, I was clean on the inside too. God is good and faithful all of the time, even when I am messing things up."

God can speak to us any time and at any place He chooses. There are times it is quite surprising when and how He speaks. While that is true, He can speak when and where He wants to, it is a good discipline to have a time and a place in which you prepare to hear from God. We should make it a specific time and place we can dedicate as a time to read, meditate, pray, contemplate, be silent and listen for the voice of the Lord. He typically does not speak while we are reading our emails and text messages from the night before, so we must position ourselves giving God our full attention ready to hear.

Awake for Intimacy

He wakens me looking for fellowship and the place of intimacy (see Isaiah 50:4). He wakes and stirs typically in a most gentle way. So gentle that if I am looking for sleep more than I am looking for God, then sleep I will. We should ask God for a heart to hear Him more than we have an appetite for eggs and bacon. Dallas Willard explains, "The gentleness of God's approach, God's spiritual invasions into human life seem, by their very gentleness, to invite us to explain them away" (282). In other words, if we are more tuned into our wishes of sleep and food, we can miss that God is desirous of spending time with us. Proverbs 8:32-35 invites:

> Now then, my children, listen to Me; blessed are those who keep My ways. Listen to My instruction and be wise; do not disregard it. Blessed are those who listen to Me, watching *daily* at My doors, *waiting* at My doorway...[emphasis mine].

It is important to note that some of us are not wired for mornings, we think that if God wanted us to see sunrises He would have planned them later in the day and we are most alert in the evening. Whether you are wired for mornings or evening, just understand the importance of finding intimacy. God will never force us to spend time with Him. It is the nature of love and of intimacy to choose to be with our Gentle Shepherd.

In this place where we have positioned ourselves to hear, spend plenty of time feeding on God's Word. Invite the Holy Spirit to teach you what it means. Remember He loves to teach, so when you pray ask, "Holy Spirit what does this mean?" Psalm 119:11 says, "I have hidden [stored up] Your word in my heart that I might not sin against You" [emphasis mine]. The more we hide the Word of God in our hearts the more we will be able to discern the Lord's voice above any other.

Positioning ourselves to hear from God in intimacy is different than positioning ourselves for a solution. Intimacy is important in that some of us have difficulty in hearing partly because what we want to hear is different from actually hearing what God would like us to hear. We are listening only for instructions or answers, when what He wants is a conversation of thoughts and ideas or our gaze of worship and praise. Intimacy is a very emotional, private confidence shared between two parties. Intimacy creates a longing to hear.

Great Listening Advice from Habakkuk
The prophet Habakkuk provides a great model for us in learning to hear from God. Habakkuk boldly asked God deep questions and verbalized his concerns and had an unwavering faith that God would answer. Habakkuk did not ask out of whining or complaining, he asked out of a heart of compassion and a desire for justice for God's people. God answered his inquiries. When God answers our questions, it is seldom to just give us knowledge or information. With revelation action is required. Upon receiving God's answers Habakkuk responded with prayers of faith.

Habakkuk says, "I will stand at my watch and station myself on the ramparts; I will look to see what He will say to me" (Habakkuk 2:1). The prophet is putting himself in a position to hear. "The watchman and watchtower" is a phrase often used by the prophets to show an attitude of expectation (Isaiah 21:8, 11; Jeremiah 6:17; Ezekiel 3:17). Habakkuk was putting himself in the best position possible to hear. This was a familiar place for Habakkuk, "I will climb to *my* [emphasis mine] watchtower." To hear best we should cultivate a place that is comfortable and familiar. A place where we can fix our eyes and ears upon God free from other distractions. A place where we can experience intimacy with God. It might be a place outdoors, a mountain peak or on a big rock near a stream. It might be a place indoors, a cozy chair with preferred light where we can nestle down to listen for the voice of the Lord.

Habakkuk says he "stationed" (see Habakkuk 2:1), himself there. Stationed implies he situated himself to wait with patience to hear from God. While God can speak anyway and anytime He wants to, we miss His voice and the revelation He wants to bring into our lives because we are often too rushed. Habakkuk was not hurried or rushed; he was stationed for the duration. There was nothing more important than hearing God's answer. We are so conditioned for the hurried and quick. Twenty second commercials and microwave ovens have become our standard. We seldom understand the importance of abiding and waiting. We often live too hurried to cultivate our spiritual hearing. Like Habakkuk, set aside enough time in our lives that we can regularly "station" ourselves before God.

When the Lord replied to Habakkuk's question, He gave him a specific instruction as a part of the answer in Habakkuk 2:2-3 (NLT):

> Write My answer plainly on tablets, so that a runner can carry the correct message to others. This vision is for a future time. It describes the end, and it will be fulfilled. If it seems slow in coming, wait patiently, for it will surely take place. It will not be delayed.

When we experience the Lord's voice it is important to write down what He says. Keep a journal of these times with God which helps us remember and serves as documentation of something

God has revealed. We should take enough time to write it plainly so we or another can read what we wrote at some future date. It is important to write down revelations from God whether dreams, visions or thoughts that are impressed on our hearts because it is so human to forget over time what God said. God indicates His answer to Habakkuk is an answer that would be needed for some future date. It needed to be written down because someone beside Habakkuk would need to read it.

Ready Yourself to Hear
The Lord does not hold us at a distance, and neither should we hold God at a distance when it relates to His presence. He desires to come near to us. He wants to hear our voice, He wants us to listen to His voice, but most of all He longs to be with us. When we are intimate with someone, we can take long drives without either party saying anything, their presence is enough. The Lord's presence is enough to revitalize our hearts and help us live our day knowing we are loved by Abba, God.

When we position ourselves to hear, we are positioning ourselves for fresh strength. Isaiah 40:31 (NKJV) says, "But those who wait on the Lord shall renew their strength; they shall mount up with wings like eagles, they shall run and not be weary, they shall walk and not faint." Each new day is a time for fresh strength, to renew our strength, because all of our strength from yesterday is used up.

We should not be surprised when God wakes us in the night. This is especially true If our hearts are continually available to Him. I have been awakened more during those times when I have said to God, "Lord I am available to pray or to fellowship with You whenever You choose. 2 Chronicles 16:9 says, "For the eyes of the Lord range throughout the earth to strengthen those whose hearts are fully committed to Him." The study notes in the Fire Bible (MEV) says, "God sees the difference between those whose hearts are completely devoted to Him and whose affections are divided between Him and the world" (571). Some of the sweetest times of fellowship are in the middle of the night.

God knows when our hearts are positioned and ready to hear and listen to His voice. Jack Deere in his fine book *Surprised by the Voice of God* writes:

> "When God sees that in our heart of hearts we are truly willing to do whatever He says, He will speak to us...I think that God often refrains from speaking to us in His mercy because He knows we would disobey His voice and bring judgement upon ourselves" (314).

Could it be true that there are times when God does not speak simply because we are not positioned or ready to walk in obedience to His voice? He does not want us to bring judgment on ourselves by grieving the Holy Spirit (see Ephesians 4:30). He loves us so much that He is even protecting us through His silence.

Positioning Yourself in Prayer
Romans 8:26-27 speaks of the fact that there are times when we do not know how to pray as we ought. This passage speaks of intimacy as it says, "The Spirit Himself intercedes for us through wordless groans." When we are in His presence as He intercedes for us, there is this wonderful connection between the Father (Who knows the mind of the Spirit), Jesus who is also interceding, the Holy Spirit and ourselves. What does this have to do with hearing? If we stop praying because we do not know what to pray for, we are missing a most meaningful time of interaction with the Godhead; The Three in One. God often speaks in this moment of silent prayer as it is a moment of meekness when we are admitting, we do not know what to do. God speaks when we are yielded to His Spirit. If we think about it, our prayerlessness is a form of arrogance in that we are saying to God since we do not know what to pray, we must not need to pray.

Some of us just keep on speaking, thinking it is praying but we are either complaining to God or praying misdirected prayers. Jesus warned us in Matthew 6:7 "And when you pray, do not keep on babbling like pagans, for they think they will be heard because of their many words." It would be so much better to be quiet and invite the Holy Spirit to pray through us.

Hearing in Stressful Times
In writing of finding a time and place and using a journal, I am not in any way suggesting that is the only time God will speak to us. There are times we cannot go to our comfy place and wait upon God. He is a merciful God Who also speaks out of our brokenness and out of our times of pressure and stress. During crisis times God is faithful to us to speak loudly and in such a way that we know it is God coming to our aid and rescue.

I do believe that when we have positioned ourselves regularly to hear from God it makes it easier to pick up the sound of His voice in the crisis moment. Having spent time with God and His Word gives us a reservoir of strength, promises and peace from which to draw on during those times when it seems that all hell is breaking loose against us.

Points to Ponder
A note about journaling: I have never been great about keeping a diary style of journal, but I find jotting down my dreams, words I have heard from God, prophecies that have been given over my life, and promises that I sense are for me is an invaluable resource. I go to that notebook often to bring to remembrance what God has spoken to my heart. This always serves as a great encouragement to me. Whether you are prolific in your journaling or an occasional jotter like me, let's join Habakkuk in writing down what the Lord has spoken.

What lessons do you draw from the Habakkuk story?

Focus for Prayer: *Abba, Father, I desire to be available to You even if it is at a time that would seem inconvenient to me. I do not want to miss one moment of the intimacy of hearing Your voice.*

Chapter 11 – Humility - The Secret to Hearing

Hearing His Voice

Ssebunya Kennedy founder of Beautiful Feet Orphanage in Uganda says: *"My parents died in an accident when I was 6 years old. I was left with my brother and sister and we started living with our grandma after none of our other relatives wanted to take us into their homes. In 2005 my brother died of HIV AIDS and then in 2007 my sister Allison died and in 2009 my grandmother died also. As a result, I was living in depression and I thought that am also going to die. I was crying and went three days without eating. I heard a voice up from the roof that said, 'YOU WILL NOT DIE MY SON, YOU HAVE ALOT TO WITNESS.' I looked around to see who was talking to me but I didn't see anyone."*

"The second time I heard God's voice very clearly was in 2018 when we were caring for 52 orphans. A part of our small building collapsed taking the lives of four children. Those who were helping with the orphans ran away because they didn't want to be part of the problem, so I was left alone with the kids. Discouraged with nowhere to go, I also thought of leaving because I was overwhelmed and there did not seem to be anything that I could do for the remaining children. I heard a voice whispering to me saying that 'I AM GOING TO PROVIDE, DON'T LEAVE MY CHURCH BEHIND.' I wondered why me? But I determined that I must listen and obey God no matter how bad the situation is. Today we are caring for 89 orphans and God has provided a shelter for the children through Wayne a man I have never met face to face."

When my son was in kindergarten, he came home after being in school for about four weeks and confidently announced. "I am not going back!" His mother, concerned that something might have happened at school, asked him "why not?" With the assurance of a five-year-old, he answered, "Because I already knows just about ebreething." It is hard to learn and to hear when we deceptively believe we already know just about everything. Herein, lies one of the great secrets to hearing God's voice.

Humility Attracts
I do not draw doctrine from the foil of Dove chocolates, but while savoring the chocolate, I always look at the, mostly, cheesy messages on the back of the foil. A recent Dove message said, "Your vibe attracts your tribe." There is some truth in that. We tend to attract people like ourselves. Jesus is humble in heart and the people most likely to hear the voice of the humble Savior clearly and correctly are those who walk with a humble spirit. As Bill Johnson so powerfully says, "Humility is the heart condition that attracts God's voice into your situation" (49).

Humility has a teachable spirit and consequently longs to hear the voice of the Spirit. Humility says I have few answers and I desperately need to hear God's voice. James 4:6 says, "God opposes the proud but shows favor to the humble." Humility is the quality that opens the way for God to work in our lives.

The word humble in the Greek is *tapeinos* means "low estate". A person of "low estate" walks and lives with the awareness that apart from Christ we can do nothing of significance, importance, or value (see John 15:5). Apart from Jesus we have no hope of bearing fruit in our lives. Humility is an attitude of heart where we earnestly want what He wants for us, so we keep out of His way, not hindering His work in us but quietly believing He will perform it. Humility is not to be confused with self-esteem where we think less of ourselves, it is thinking of and promoting ourselves less.

There is a vast difference between humility and humiliation, the two words come from the same root word, but they are different. Being humble is an attitude choice we make while humiliation refers to something that happens to us, such as a situation or life event that is considered shameful or brings us a sense of dishonor.

Being humble is not easy, if it was there would be more humble people. Humility requires application of God's strengthening grace in our lives. Many of us have a wrong idea about humility, thinking it means we grovel in front of others, seeing ourselves as a doormat where we put ourselves and others down. Humility is not thinking more highly of ourselves than we should (see Romans 12:3). Humility is being comfortable with who we are in Christ and understanding we are His handiwork (Ephesians 2:10). In humility we do not have anything to prove, it is gratefully walking in God's strength and grace.

Jesus and The Holy Spirit Reveal Humility
Everything in Jesus life including His birth speaks of humility. Jack Deere says: "The birth of Jesus teaches us that the humble will be the first to hear the voice of God. Whether driven to it through desperate circumstances or having acquired it through careful cultivation, the quality of humility is essential for hearing the voice of God"(40). Jesus was not only born in humility; He lived His life in humility. He was meek with no pretensions. Matthew 11:28-29 says, "Come to Me, all you who are weary and burdened, and I will give you rest. Take My yoke upon you and learn from Me, for I am gentle and humble in heart, and you will find rest for your souls." John 1:1 says, "In the beginning was the Word, and the Word was with God, and the Word was God." The Son who was in the beginning with God, laid equality with God aside (see Philippians 2:6-7) out of His love for us and out of our desperate need of a Savior.

The Holy Spirit is a humble Spirit. His presence is likened to a dove. We see a wonderful picture of this humility at Jesus baptism. John the Baptizer gave this testimony, "I saw the Spirit come down from heaven as a dove and remain on Him" (John 1:32). The Dove could remain and rest on Jesus because there was nothing in the heart of Jesus to scare the Dove away.

As mentioned in the last chapter, the humble Holy Spirit can be grieved, which is why we are called to "..rid ourselves of bitterness, rage, and anger, brawling and slander, along with every form of malice" (Ephesians 4:31). The Dove does not rest upon us the children of God when we walk outside of the way of love and humility.

Both Jesus and the Holy Spirit reveal the spirit of humility. Jesus is humble, saying, I can do nothing apart from the Father (see John 5:19). The Holy Spirit is humble, He does no self-promotion, He simply and continually points to Jesus. In fact we grieve the Holy Spirit when we fail to take Jesus seriously.

The Moses Model of Humility
Moses had a wife that his siblings Aaron and Miriam did not approve of. Out of their critical attitude they became jealous of the way that God was using their brother Moses. They asked of God, "Is Moses the only one You talk through?" There is one verse that gives a clue as to why God used Moses to the degree He did, "(Now Moses was a very humble man, more humble than anyone else on the face of the earth)" (Numbers 12:3). The verse was probably added after Moses' death by his servant Joshua, which is why it is in parentheses. God desires the intimacy He had with Moses with each of us. Scripture says of this man of humility: "With him I speak face to face" (Numbers 12:8). God loved Moses so much that even his funeral showed God's intimate relationship with Moses. God made all of Moses' funeral arrangements and buried Moses Himself; no one was invited to the funeral.

Dallas Willard offers commentary:
> Miriam and Aaron wanted God to legitimize their position,

insisting that He spoke to them also. But they weren't in tune with what God wanted done, but only with what they wanted done...Humility is a quality that opens the way for God to work because God resists the proud (1 Peter 5: 5)(51). This is a good reminder to be cautious against complaining about how God might be using someone else. God asked, Aaron and Miriam, "Why were you not afraid to speak against my servant Moses?" (Numbers 12:8). Our complaints always show a lack of gratitude and a lack of gratitude is tied to an arrogant spirit.

Moses is an example of the kind of person that God uses and blesses. God uses and blesses those He can trust, who will steward assignments well. Walking in humility, comfortable with who we are in God, is surely a sign to God we are trustworthy. Moses did not start out this way, remember when God called him, he had many inferiorities. Moses told God that he was not good enough for the task because he did not talk eloquently. God does not withdraw His calling or assignment because we do not know how or we feel inadequate. Moses developed intimacy with God as he learned God's voice and learned to walk in dependency on God.

Developing a Spirit of Humility
One of the keys to developing the fruit of humility in our lives is to turn our attention away from ourselves to God's magnificence. Job's anguish and grief provide an interesting example. His three friends came to offer comfort in his grief. Things went pretty well when they sat with Job in silence for seven days and nights. No one said a word. It was when they all started talking that perspective was lost. Thirty-eight chapters later, God starts pointing them to the wonders of His power and the grandeur of His creation. Out of hearing God's voice, Job said, "Surely, I spoke of things I did not understand, things too wonderful for me to know" (Job 42:3). This perspective is what happens to all of us when we in humility listen to the Lord.

Humility is so important in hearing the voice of God because in humility we neither try to impress God with what we know or how desperate our need. Humility is the deep hunger to be in His presence knowing that when He speaks, we want to hear carefully what has just been spoken. I love having impressions, whispers, and thoughts from God, because almost always the thoughts are extraordinary. So much so that I know I was not smart enough to think the thought by myself.

Humility Seeks Permission
When God begins to speak to us and we are beginning to hear His voice clearly it is easy to be pleased, spiritually fulfilled and excited. When we are excited about something it is easy to want to tell someone else. Blurting out what we have heard from God usually is full of pride. It does not dawn on most of us that when He speaks to us, it is probably for our ears only; at least at first. Just because we have heard from God does not mean that we have His permission to share it. I wish I would have learned this lesson much earlier. Not only was the timing off, but in sharing what I did not have permission to share I grieved the Holy Spirit.

It is very presumptuous to share what we have heard without seeking the Holy Spirit's permission. I am afraid that though well-meaning there have been times I have appeared pretty full of myself in speaking what God had said before it had fully germinated in my heart and given in His appointed time. This is a definite way to still the voice of the Holy Spirit. He does not speak to those He cannot trust. When this happens, we need to repent of our impetuousness and ask for the restoration of humility.

Understanding God's Love
Understanding how much God loves us (to the degree we are able) causes a sense of humility. A J Sherrill in his profound little book *Quiet* says, "We are less important than we think, yet more loved that we know" (40). When we come to grips with how much we are loved then our self-esteem is no longer tied to our performance but our identity in Christ. I John 3:1 says, "See what great love the Father has lavished on us, that we should be called children of God! And that is what we are!"

Once I know I am loved, I do not have to establish worth by comparison or competition. Humility comes when we refuse to compare ourselves with other people. Writer of yesteryear, Andrew Murray says: "Humility is to be at rest when nobody praised me and when I am blamed or despised. It is to go in and shut the door and kneel to my Father in secret and be at peace as in the deep sea of calmness when all around and above is in trouble" (Draper's Book of Quotations, 325). Since humility is being comfortable with who we are in God, seeking our identity outside of Christ will always distort our spiritual hearing.

All of us go through humbling experiences. It is certainly better to humble ourselves than for us to continue to have to be humbled because arrogance gets us into trouble. James 4:10 says, "Humble yourselves before the Lord, and He will lift you up." Promotion, blessing, and favor come from the Lord. When the verse says He will lift us up, it means He will lift us from our old ways of doing things and make us new in Christ.

Spiritual Arrogance Repels
Pride and arrogance plug our ears from being able to clearly hear the voice of the Lord. The person who is prideful and arrogant cannot enter into intimacy with the Lord. Self-absorbed individuals find it difficult to have closeness in any relationship including the Lord. Psalm 138:6 (NLT) says, "Though the Lord is great, He cares for the humble, but He keeps His distance from the proud." Arrogance contains an attitude of superiority and entitlement, this type of self-importance creates distance between us and the Lord.

One of the more subtle forms of arrogance is self-righteousness. An attitude that says, "I may not be as good as I should be, but I am a lot better than most other people." This religious spirit is referred to by Isaiah when He says, "These people come near to Me with their mouth and honor Me with their lips, but their hearts are far from Me. Their worship of Me is based on merely human rules they have been taught" (Isaiah 29:13).

Jack Deere says, "When a person thinks they possess awesome knowledge of a sufficient Bible, they don't tend to ask God for many directions. They don't need to, because they have all the direction they ever need in their awesome knowledge of the Bible" (67). A proper understanding of the Word leads us to humility, never to self-sufficiency. With much knowledge, if we are not careful, we can get puffed up by what we know. Religiously we can know a lot of Bible and even win Bible trivia games without truly knowing Him, the One who longs to be intimate with us.

Arrogance already knows the answer or at least carries the false pretense of knowing. A religious spirit can seem so humble. Pastor Bill Johnson says:

> False humility is often seen in self-abasement, self-criticism, and self-condemnation...It is the most dangerous form of pride because it is thought of as a spiritual value, which gives it permission to stay. As such, it is guarded and protected as though it were a godly trait (226).

D.L. Moody says, "A man can counterfeit love, he can counterfeit faith, he can counterfeit hope and other graces, but is very difficult to counterfeit humility" (324). False humility will never bring us into the place of intimacy in hearing His whisper.

A spirit of humility does not spend much time focusing or even noticing the flaws of others. A harsh and critical spirit is one of the character flaws that God desires to help us grow out of through fostering the heart of humility. Speaking well of others and looking for every opportunity to serve especially when it is out of the limelight becomes really enjoyable to the person choosing and learning to have a humble heart. We can ask God to help us with developing a humble heart like Jesus.

Refusing Offense

Being too easily offended is a sign we need to humble ourselves. Holding on to an offense puts us into a role we were not designed for. Forgiving and letting go of the offense is the most Christlike thing we can do. Being unwilling to forgive always puts us in the role of arrogance, because a heart of forgiveness is born out of a spirit of humility. Not to forgive is to play God. A deep sense of thanksgiving for our own forgiveness from the Lord will help in our facilitation of forgiving others.

There are times in all our lives when we experience extreme suffering, when releasing an offense is a difficult and sometimes a long process. Very often we cannot help what happens to us but walking in comfortable intimacy with God helps us to choose what happens in us. Jesus promised us "in this world you will have trouble. But take heart! I have overcome the world" (John 16:33). There is undue suffering that occurs at the hands and because of the sinfulness of others. The "why" question haunts us and like Job who wanted answers but never really received them, life deals us tough situations. God will be faithful to each of us to bring good out of difficulties and out of the worst of offenses speak words of peace and comfort to our heart.

Romans 8:28 says, "And we know that in all things God works for the good of those who love Him, who have been called according to His purpose." The best would be for the molestation to not have occurred. The best would be if father were not addicted to alcohol and did not abuse his wife and kids. The best would be if the car accident would never have occurred. But God promises good to those who love Him. He promises that out of the worst of circumstances He will bring good to us.

Humility says God will sustain us, will help us and we can quietly listen for His whisper in the worst of circumstances. Intimacy with Abba comes through listening for and to His voice.

Points to Ponder

Why do you think a spirit of humility is so important in hearing the voice of the Lord?

Can you think of a time you had a thought you immediately knew you were not smart or clever enough to think by yourself?

Why is having a heart to hear more important than having the ability to hear?

What steps can you intentionally take over the next 4 weeks to develop that kind of humble heart?

Prayer Focus: *Lord, are there ways my pride is sabotaging my life? Please make me aware of the areas where I need to humble myself.*

Chapter 12 – Soaking in the Presence

Hearing His Voice

Matt shared: "So as a baby Christian, I had lost my eyeglasses. I spent hours, if not days, looking for them with no success. They were the only glasses I had at the time, and even though I could still see well enough without them I desperately looked everywhere. It wasn't until I finally gave up on my own and just asked God if he could please help me find my glasses. Instantly I felt him say, "Look under the passenger seat of your car." So I did, and there they were. I wish I could say that this always taught me to look to Him first, but I am still struggling to find things on my own. Looking back, I wonder if the glasses represented more than just glasses. Perhaps He wanted me to come to Him to see more clearly."

Soaking is not a hurried process whether soaking our lawn or taking a soak in the bathtub. Soaking provides a saturation, an immersion, that is not available from a drip, spray or a sprinkle. I have enjoyed growing bonsai (pronounced "bone-sigh") as a hobby. The word bonsai means "tree in a pot." The small size of bonsai trees is attained through root and branch pruning which makes the watering process more important than watering a shrub or tree in the yard. There is an art to proper watering of bonsai trees. Periodically the trees, instead of being sprinkled, need a good soaking. My method of soaking is to fill a wheelbarrow full of water and light fertilizer and fully immerse the pot containing the bonsai. Immediately air pockets bubble from the root system and are exchanged for the nutrients in the water and fertilizer. The trees are left to soak until all the air is fully out of the soil and root system.

Just as soaking is important to bonsai trees, regular soaking is important to us as believers. Taking plenty of time to spend in God's Word, in listening, adoring, treasuring, pondering, meditating, and contemplating is akin to a good soak. There is nothing wrong with quick or flash prayers and focusing on a verse or two of Scripture but that is not the same as marinating or soaking. A spiritual soak releases the toxins of the world out of our spiritual root system. This happens when we lose track of time in wonder and worship while in the presence of the Lord or in an unrushed time when the Holy Spirit speaks to us personally out of a passage of Scripture in such a way it becomes a part of our thinking.

Something deep and intimate is revealed in an unrushed soak. Something priceless within is satisfied. The availability of our hearts and longing to spend time in His presence has a lot to do with whether we experience time in absorbing His blessing and anointing. Hurrying our times with the Lord certainly will not create the kind of spiritual depth we desire in our lives or the kind of intimacy the Lord longs for with us. Abba Father desires to show us His heart and that does not happen when we are always rushing and trying to check spiritual performance boxes. To develop the mind of Christ means we spend extended periods with Him to know His heart, His priorities, and His thinking for our situations. This is so important if we are to develop keen spiritual hearing.

As a church pastor there have been worship services when I have sensed God is calling us to soak in His blessing. Times when the Holy Spirit has whispered, "today is not a day to teach or preach." It is as if He is saying, "I love the aroma of worship coming from the saints, and I want them to be able to soak up My presence." There is absolutely nothing more wonderful than those times when the Holy Spirit shows up in that kind of soaking way.

An instant gratification mindset fails to produce the depth and spiritual maturity we desire. We cannot microwave up a deeper relationship with Jesus, but there is a sense of spiritual beauty that can be developed by giving God time. I would like to explore some processes that will help our development of intimacy through hearing.

Meditation

Meditation is an important word and a Scriptural word many believers have regrettably tried to distance themselves from because of its use and connotation in eastern religions. While there are those who think of meditation as simply emptying the mind, that is not the biblical usage. Meditation means to "mull over," to "deeply ponder." The word originates from the picture of a cow chewing the cud. We use the expression for a thought that stretches our minds and we say, "I need to chew on that." God's Word is always stretching us in such a way we need to chew on it. When we ponder a thought, we may or may not talk about it, we place it away in a safe place in our hearts and then in quiet bring the thought back up to process it some more. We chew on it until it becomes a part of us, this is pondering and meditating. Psalm 1:3 (NLT) describes the results of a person who chews the things of God, "They are like trees planted along the riverbank, bearing fruit each season. Their leaves never wither, and they prosper in all they do."

Contemplation

In addition to meditation, contemplation warrants our attention as well. Contemplation is a good word, used only once in Scripture, Paul speaks of the transformative power of contemplating the Lord's glory (see 2 Corinthians 3:18). Contemplation speaks of wordless prayers with the awareness of His presence while experiencing deep intimacy with Him.

When my wife sent me letters while still in the dating process, I would read those letters over and over, holding on to every word. So important was what she wrote that I would look at every stroke of the pen and could even hear her voice as I read. Being in love meant I was captivated by her heart. Learning to know the heart of God is so precious and illuminating, it takes us away from always thinking we need to figure things out. It helps us to see our lives and every situation through the lens of His heart of love instead of the many filters we bring into our relationship with Him. This process happens as we meditate and contemplate the things of God.

Intimacy holds on to every word and whisper, it cannot be a rushed process. In contemplation we pause, we ponder and think deeply of God's plan and His purposes for our lives. In contemplation we silently listen for the voice of the Holy Spirit because "Words are inadequate to broker the kind of depth God longs for us to experience" (Quiet 61). It is in contemplation where we see the mind of Christ. We are unable to align our desires with God's plan for our lives without the mind of Christ.

In the passage of Scripture where the Apostle Paul describes having the mind of Christ, I believe He is revealing why contemplation is important. 1 Corinthians 2:9-13 (TPT) says:

> This is why the Scriptures say: Things never discovered or heard of before, things beyond our ability to imagine—these are the many things God has in store for all His lovers. But God now unveils these profound realities to us by the Spirit. Yes, He has revealed to us His inmost heart and deepest mysteries through the Holy Spirit, who constantly explores all things. After all, who can really see into a person's heart and know his hidden impulses except for that person's spirit? So it is with God. His thoughts and secrets are only fully understood by His Spirit, the Spirit of God. For we did not receive the spirit of this world system but the Spirit of God, so that we might come to understand and experience all that grace has lavished upon us. And we articulate these realities with the words imparted to us by the Spirit and not with the words taught by human wisdom. We join together Spirit-revealed truths with Spirit-revealed words.

We must soak up what God reveals to us in His whispers and impressions with the Holy Spirit's help. Often when God speaks to us, there is a follow up question on our part, such as, is what You just spoke for a later date? Is there something I am supposed to do right now as a result of what You have spoken? When God whispers to us it is as if He is telling a secret to a trusted friend and we need to understand the timing of what He has spoken. How wonderful to contemplate God's Word but also what He has whispered to us.

Cease Doing All the Talking

We can never learn the heart of God when we do all the talking. It is a dysfunctional relationship when one person does all the talking. What makes us think the relationship with God is any different? No wonder we do not find intimacy. In the sparse time we find for relationship building, we do not stop talking long enough for God to get a word in edge wise. Henri Nouwen says, "as long as our hearts and minds are filled with words of our own making, there is no space for the word to enter deeply in our heart and take root" (97). How liberating to know that we can come into the presence of the Lord knowing He knows all about us and passionately loves us and calls us into a depth of intimacy we have not known.

God Initiated Times

We know God first initiated our relationship with Him. We could not and would not have known we even needed Him in our lives without His initiation. After we give our hearts to the Lord and have the assurance that we are His child something seems to shift for many to where we see ourselves as primary initiators of the intimacy. Mercifully, we can present to Abba all of our needs, but if we are not careful the relationship becomes needs driven instead of motivated by nothing more than being with God in companionship. Why do we think our needs should set the agenda? Should our prayer list, as important as it is to us, set the agenda? The answers for all things flow out of Who He is. It is so much richer and deeper when, instead of seeking the answers, we seek Him. Out of seeking Him, the answers will come with His perfect timing. In this we find peace because we are not begging Him or praying in fear, we are with Him, and in being with Him we are learning His heart.

I am not suggesting that we not worry about the disciplines of prayer or a quiet time. Those disciplines are important and wonderful. The quiet place of devotion is often a place and time of hearing God's voice. I am simply suggesting that our hearts are so in tune with His heart and voice that He can initiate the moments He wants to meet with us. We want to learn to hear His invitation so we can hear His heart and hear the partnership to which He might be calling us. What I am suggesting is that we learn to abide in His presence, in awareness of Him.

Abiding
Jesus said to His disciples in John 15:4 (NKJV), "Abide in Me, and I in you. As the branch cannot bear fruit of itself, unless it abides in the vine, neither can you, unless you abide in Me." We do not use the word "abide" much anymore. It is a good word that conveys being at home in an abode. Some translations use the word "remain" in place of the word "abide." I believe it weakens the text, because the concept of abiding is not just hanging out as friends but exchanging life. Jesus is saying "It is the man who shares My life and whose life I share who proves fruitful" (J.B.Phillips).

There are friendships when one party stays stagnant and stuck and stops growing while the other is growing, setting goals and taking risk. Not too many months go by where there is little to talk about in that relationship. It is a draining relationship. Other relationships when two friends are on the same page, after time spent together there is a sense of an invigoration and a fulfillment.

Time with Him brings peace, rest and a sense of safety. Just as a preschool teacher uses a quiet voice to tone down a noisy room,

God whispers to us to still the noise within. In His presence silence is safe. Sometimes we are afraid that in silence the secrets of our hearts will be laid bare, but how else can those things be healed? God knows all about us and still considers us His precious children, even calling us friends. In the quiet place we can be emptied of anything that would hinder and in that moment of intimacy the Dove of Heaven will come to rest upon us as He did Jesus at His baptism and abide.

This abiding presence of God is a place of rest, a garden of safety and repose where we learn His heart for us, where we learn what He values, and we learn to share in the priorities and values of heaven. Out of heart intimacy we not only start thinking of His heart, we develop the desire to start praying and acting from His heart. It is out of abiding in His presence we receive the promise of John 15:7 (NKJV) "If you abide in Me, and My words abide in you, you will ask what you desire, and it shall be done for you." This promise is totally true because out of the intimacy of knowing His heart, out of sharing life together I desire what He desires.

Gazing and Adoration
A great illustration of intimacy is seen in the story of Luke 10 where Jesus shows up at the home of Mary and Martha. Martha is busy in the kitchen trying to make sure that everything is tasty, presentable, and fit for the King visiting their home. Readers are often a little hard on Martha, she was trying to do the right thing. But sometimes serving the Lord can get in the way of intimacy. Mary sat at the feet of Jesus gazing into His presence, adoring His company, receiving life from every word He spoke. Martha in her service only caught glimpses. Mary gazed. Mary soaked. When we gaze, we are not distracted and we are unhurried. When we gaze at someone we love we lose track of time.

Another story that speaks to us of sitting at the feet of Jesus is found in Mark 14:3, "While He was in Bethany, reclining at the table in the home of Simon the Leper, a woman came with an alabaster jar of very expensive perfume, made of pure nard. She broke the jar and poured the perfume on His head." This woman is having a most blessed worship experience. She is anointing Jesus with the most expensive, fragrant perfume.

Judas and others are simply spectators and are irritated by this act of adoration. Jesus and the woman are blessed as she is having a worship experience. I have noticed the same thing happens in churches, the ones who come to spectate usually leave irritated and those who break something of themselves open and gaze at the Master and adore Him are blessed. **The fragrance of the woman's worship filled the whole house.**

To adore Abba is to treasure and prize Him. With an unrushed gaze we will cherish Him and praise Him. When we honor Him, we release a sacrifice of ourselves to Him. And in these intimate times of abiding with Abba Father there is a divine exchange of His life for our brokenness and His presence brings healing.

Delighting
Delighting in the Lord is another word to familiarize ourselves with. We kind of skim right over those passages using this word because we are not quite sure what delighting looks like. Delighting is a lot like a reunion. Reunions are so fun to watch because there is such delight. Seeing the eyes and smiles of families when their soldier comes home from deployment is so heartwarming. The faces of a grandparent and grandchild when they see each other after an absence shows delight. When we delight ourselves in the Lord, it is like the privilege of running into His arms each day thrilled that I get to be with Abba, Father. When this is our attitude, Psalm 37:4 says, "Delight yourself also in the Lord, And He shall give you the desires of your heart."

What is exciting about intimacy with the Lord is we are not the only one who enjoys the relationship when we delight in Him. The Lord delights in us as well. He cannot wait for us to wake up in the morning to have fellowship with us and make Himself better known to us. Isaiah 50:4-5 says, "He wakens me morning by morning, wakens my ear to listen like one being instructed. The Sovereign Lord has opened my ears; I have not been rebellious; I have not turned away." He delights in us so much that He has our name engraved on the palm of His hands (see Isaiah 49:16).

Patience in The Soak
Soaking in God's presence whether in meditation, contemplation, abiding or whatever listening posture He calls us is always time well spent. We will not find intimacy or learn to know His heart without taking time to absorb and assimilate what He wants to say to us. Soaking allows what we have heard to mature in our hearts.

Earlier I mentioned the art of raising bonsai trees. Bonsai brings horticulture and art together. The art is satisfying because the tree cannot be rushed, only cultivated, nurtured, and provided the right micro-climate for proper growth. A good artist spends much time with the tree envisioning where to prune. This is not a rushed process because once a branch is cut off it cannot be put back. Such a contemplative process requires patience and time. It can easily take five to ten years for a bonsai tree to take shape.

I see some parallels in John 15, where Jesus speaks of the Father as the gardener. Our Heavenly Gardener desires us to grow and thrive. He prunes off that which is not beneficial so that we can be more fruitful. He tenderly helps us soak to receive the spiritual nutrients for us to flourish. He compassionately cultivates away any weeds that hinder us from receiving intimacy through His voice.

Points to Ponder
If you are finding it difficult to make time to soak in His presence. I would encourage you to plan a day away with God simply for a

good soak.

What has God said that you need to contemplate or meditate upon?

Focus for Prayer: *Father, teach me to slow down in our times together. Thank you for freeing me from the necessity of me doing all of the talking. I want to be a better listener in our relationship!*

Chapter 13 – Hearing for the Sake of Encouraging Others

Hearing His Voice

One of our ministry team members writes:
"One Sunday during prayer time after church a lady came up to me and asked for prayer concerning a situation in her life. I had never experienced what she was talking about and couldn't think of any Scriptures speaking to her situation, so I just began praying general prayers for wisdom and discernment. Then I stopped speaking and just listened to the Holy Spirit, hoping for something that would help this woman. I didn't hear words but an idea or impression came to my mind. I opened my eyes and said to the woman, 'I'm not sure if this is from my own thoughts (because I so badly wanted to hear something) or from the Spirit so if it resonates with your spirit, take it. If not, let it go.' I closed my eyes and began praying specifically to the situation in line with the impression I had about it. When I finished I opened my eyes to find the woman staring at me, eyes wide with a big smile on her face. "That's exactly what the Lord has been telling me. I will keep pressing forward until I see a breakthrough!' Then she hugged me and went away full of encouragement. A week or two later she told me that she experienced breakthrough and the situation was resolved."

Once we begin learning to hear the voice of the Lord, He will speak to us for the sake of encouraging others. People are so full of discouragement that they need a fresh dose of courage. Both the word "encourage," and the word "discourage," have the word "courage" tucked neatly inside. Discourage is to take courage out and encourage is to put courage in. God often speaks to us so that we in turn can put courage in another person. Hebrews 3:13 says, "But encourage one another daily, as long as it is called 'Today,' so that none of you may be hardened by sin's deceitfulness." He loves to speak to us so that we can speak comfort, gentleness, and peace to another person.

Prophetic Encouragement
The New Testament brought a major shift in prophecy. While the Old Testament model was forthtelling and foretelling and in many cases pronouncing judgement, the model of the New Testament is full of encouragement. Prophetic encouragement is developing the ability to see people the way that God sees them and calling them into their greatness. 1 Corinthians 14:3 gives guidelines for an impression or a word for another person, it says: "But he who prophesies speaks edification and exhortation and comfort to men." In other words, we are called to build up, stir up and cheer others up. Prophetic encouragement in the New Testament never goes outside of these boundaries. The goal of New Testament prophecy is always to bring each of us in the Body of Christ into greater intimacy with Abba, Father.

We put courage in another's heart through prophetic encouragement. God can trust us when we walk in humility and the fullness of the Spirit to speak comfort and strength to others. Kris Vallotton in his book Basic Training for the Prophetic Ministry says, "We can only prophesy to the degree that we hear and discern God's voice" (61).

In the New Testament not everyone is a prophet, but everyone can prophesy. Peter repeated the prophet Joel's words in Acts 2:17-18:
> In the last days, God says, 'I will pour out My Spirit on all people. Your sons and daughters will prophesy, your young men will see visions, your old men will dream dreams. Even

on My servants, both men and women, I will pour out My Spirit in those days, and they will prophesy.'

Paul encouraged all believers to love others and to eagerly desire the gifts of the Spirit especially prophecy (see 1 Corinthians 14:1). We are reticent to ask for any gift, but the Apostle Paul encourages us to ask for the gift of prophecy. When we understand that this gift is not for us but for the people who need the encouragement, we realize that it is not selfish to ask. Even Moses celebrated when the Spirit fell on his followers and they prophesied. Moses said, I wish that all the Lord's people were prophets and that the Lord would put his Spirit on them" (Numbers 11:29).

Hearing in Prayer
As believers we need to carefully listen during prayer times when God places a name on our hearts. He does so for specific reasons. It may be to simply pray for them, but we should ask the Holy Spirit is there something He wants us to say to them or some way He wants us to reach out to them? Their name may have been placed on our hearts for a specific assignment.

God longs to speak to us and through us as tools calling out destiny and potential in others even if that is just to pray and nothing more. As He places their name on our hearts it is to call out His image in them. Therefore, when we pray for others we must not pray in a critical spirit or judgmental attitude. We should ask God to give us a spirit of humility as we pray. Psalm 25:14 says, "The Lord confides in those who fear Him; He makes His covenant known to them."

Permission to Share
As mentioned earlier some of the words that God shares with us on behalf of others is so that we can pray. Some of these thoughts He impresses on our hearts for others are seeds of preparation that He is using our prayers to help germinate. Jack Deere says:
> I believe that the majority of dreams, impressions and visions we receive are meant to lead us to pray and not to do

anything else. The greatest prophetic people I know see and hear far more from the Lord than they ever speak. They are men and women who spend a great deal of their time in prayer (194).

We should never assume that just because we receive a revelation that we have permission to share it. A good rule of thumb is never to share anything we hear from God without first asking the Holy Spirit for His permission of when and where it may be shared. Some things are for our hearing only.

Share with Humility

We need to be careful in too freely sharing our opinions. When we receive a word for another person, that word must be spoken in humility. We must be cautious against being too cavalier. I guard against this in a couple of ways. If I sense that God has spoken or impressed something on my heart to be given to another person, when I share the word with them, I never say, "I am 100 percent sure of it!" God is never wrong but my hearing can be wrong. I tend to say something like, "I believe God has spoken to me about xyz, I am about 60 percent sure, but there is a 40 percent chance it could just be from me, not God." The percentage may change based on my discernment and based on the circumstances. The second thing I do is I ask the person I am encouraging, "does this resonate with you?" If it does great, I move ahead then pray and visit about it further. If it does not resonate with them, I suggest they put it on a shelf in case it ever does ring true with them, or trash it altogether. These two safeguards help me not to get too full of myself as I am seeking to minister to another person.

A Word of Knowledge

There are times as we are ministering to another person that the Holy Spirit may provide an insight that the person we are sharing with is aware of but could not be made known to us except by the voice of the Holy Spirit. An example of this, I was sharing my faith with a man I had met earlier. As I shared my testimony with Him, I kept hearing a man's name in my spirit. I was hearing the name so strongly that I finally asked my friend, "Does the name John (not the real name) mean anything to you? Surprised he replied, "Yes that is my Dad!" Then the Holy Spirit impressed on me that He could never please or gain his father's approval. So I asked him, "Did you feel you could never do enough to please your Dad?" He answered that that was the case. I shared with Him the Good News that through Jesus he could live in a way that would be pleasing to God. My new friend wonderfully came to know Jesus that day.

God loves to speak to us in order to call people into a relationship with Himself. He desires to call out their potential and give them hope for a wonderful future. As we learn to have intimacy with God through hearing His voice, ask the Lord if there is a word or a message He wants to give to you for encouraging another person.

A Word of Adjustment
There may be times God reveals something in another person that could be a stumbling block to them or to others. There are biblical times for reproof and correction. Galatians 6:1 gives careful guidelines, "Brothers and sisters, if someone is caught in a sin, you who live by the Spirit should restore that person gently. But watch yourselves, or you also may be tempted." The point of restoration is helping people to see the heart of the Father toward them.

When the Lord gives us an insight, or if a word of encouragement is impressed on our heart to give to another person it is seldom terse or judgmental, after all any judgment is not our department. So, if we are thinking an unkind word toward someone and we think we are supposed to share it with them, we should ask for clarification not once or twice. Many have errantly gotten into the flesh through a corrective or an unkind word spoken to another person.

Jesus warns us in Matthew 7:1-3 "Do not judge, or you too will be judged. For in the same way you judge others, you will be judged, and with the measure you use, it will be measured to you. Why do you look at the speck of sawdust in your brother's eye and pay no attention to the plank in your own eye?" Before ever thinking about offering reproof or correction to another person, we need to check our own hearts. Is the fruit of the Spirit flowing in our hearts? Time and time again I have seen people judge someone harshly only to have the same sin they are trying to correct come to roost in their own life or family. Francis Frangipane says, "We must learn to view life not with the graceless mind of a fault-finder but with the compassionate mind of the Redeemer" (11). God never gives us discernment to judge, but to offer grace, compassion, help and prayer.

Speaking Hope
The person who understands intimacy through hearing looks for divine appointments. Opportunities to partner with God through encouraging the discouraged and disillusioned. To speak into the lives of believers who are stuck. To speak hope into hopeless situations. To offer love, acceptance and forgiveness to those who feel they are never good enough and to those who have bought into the lies of the accuser that they will never measure up.

The days ahead need encouragement from the voices of prophetic believers who have heard the voice of God. Paul gives a great word of encouragement in Philippians 2:1-3 (TPT):
> Look at how much encouragement you've found in your relationship with the Anointed One! You are filled to overflowing with His comforting love. You have experienced a deepening friendship with the Holy Spirit and have felt His tender affection and mercy. So I'm asking you, my friends, that you be joined together in perfect unity—with one heart, one passion, and united in one love. Walk together with one harmonious purpose and you will fill my heart with unbounded joy. Be free from pride-filled opinions, for they will

only harm your cherished unity. Don't allow self-promotion to hide in your hearts, but in authentic humility put others first and view others as more important than yourselves.

Put on your listening ears to hear what God might want to say to you for another. Ask God to help you speak to the greatness of God in each person and call it out!

∞∞∞

Points to Ponder

Read 1 Corinthians 14:1. Why do you think Paul tells us to earnestly desire the gifts of the Spirit, especially prophecy?

Why is it important to see others as God sees them?

Reminder: Our aim in hearing prophetically is to look for the image and likeness of God inside of people and speak to that.

Focus for Prayer: *Teach me to hear responsibly that I might be an encouragement to someone else.*

Concluding Thoughts...

Margaret, one of my faithful intercessors, prayed profoundly when she prayed, "We are prepared to listen to lies and fear because we have not learned to listen to You." At the beginning of this journey I described spiritually stuck mindsets. I believe learning to hear and listen to the voice of God is the way forward for both spiritually aware and complacent and stuck believers. God longs to have intimacy with us, He wants us to know not only His voice, but His heart. He will help us quiet every other voice including the voice of failure and the voice that says "you will never be enough."

Many believers have self-imposed deafness simply because they do not expect that they can hear. When Isaiah heard the angels calling to one another in the temple the vibrations were much greater than a drum concert, at the sound of their voices the thresholds shook. Isaiah said, "Then I heard the voice of the Lord saying, 'whom shall I send? And who will go for us?" (Isaiah 6:8). Isaiah is on assignment from the Lord to tell us not only to hear, but to listen because without listening we cannot understand the heart of God. Unbelief causes heart callouses that make our ears and hearing dull. "Otherwise they might see with their eyes and hear with their ears and understand with their hearts and turn and be healed" (Isaiah 6:10). We can get unstuck spiritually when we understand that God wants to activate our hearing, for the sake of intimacy. We were created with the ability to hear and listen to God's voice. While we could not come into relationship with God apart from Him speaking and drawing us. The ability to hear grows and develops as a part of being made a new creation in Christ Jesus through the new birth. When we lean into His whisper we learn to love the sound of His voice, but even more we love Him and the privilege of being in His presence.

God is inviting us into His presence on a consistent basis so we can learn to listen to every fresh Word that proceeds out of the mouth of God. God longs to show us morning by morning and day by day His mercies, secrets of the kingdom and to reveal more and more of Himself to us. Regular time with God is transformational. This intimacy is described so well in the song *Goodness of God* sung by Jenn Johnson:

>I love You Lord
>Oh Your mercy never fails me
>All my days
>I've been held in Your hands
>From the moment that I wake up
>Until I lay my head
>I will sing of the goodness of God
>
>All my life You have been faithful
>All my life You have been so, so good
>With every breath that I am able
>I will sing of the goodness of God
>
>I love Your voice
>You have led me through the fire
>In darkest nights
>You are close like no other
>I've known You as a father
>I've known You as a friend
>I have lived in the goodness of God
>(used by permission).

This song refreshes my heart, and reminds me of Jesus words in John 15:15, "I no longer call you servants, because a servant does not know his master's business. Instead, I have called you friends for everything that I learned from my Father I have made known to you."

God longs to reveal His heart to us. He wants to reveal how we can be more like Jesus. We should let Him know that we not only want to hear Him, but we want to listen and humble ourselves in obedience to what He says. We can tell God we long for a deep and intimate connection with His voice. We can be assured He will answer that prayer.

As you read the stories of common ordinary people to whom God speaks, not only in the Scriptures but the "Hearing His Voice" stories in this book, may your heart be opened to His whisper. May you lean into Him to hear His peace, His stillness, and His heartbeat.

Pray With Me:

Lord I thank You that I was created with the ability and the desire to hear Your voice! Learning to walk in the dependency of hearing You is a part of the privilege of being made a new creation through the new birth. I thank you for Your patience with me as I am learning to hear and listen to Your whisper. Lord, I long for a deep and intimate relationship with You. The kind of relationship through which my spiritual ears are cleared of everything but Your voice. I rejoice that in Your grace You will speak to me in such a way that I can hear and understand what You are saying to my heart. I declare that as I hear Your voice, I will walk in obedience to what You say, knowing You have my best interest at heart. Thank You for hearing my prayer. In Jesus Name! Amen.

Intimacy Through Hearing

More Hearing His Voice Stories:

Phil said, "What has changed my life is slowing down and just listening to the Holy Spirit. Hearing Him has changed my life."

§

Bob Moore, a rancher in Northern Wyoming, used to laughingly tell his wife, "say a prayer for me" as she left for church. In 1990, God answered his wife's prayer in a powerful way as Bob was miraculously born again. Bob quickly became a faithful attender with his wife. The only church in this very small town struggled to keep their doors open and struggled in getting someone to teach the Word week after week. This struggle went on for nine years. The people believed the doors of the church were to stay open, so they earnestly prayed. One morning Bob, who was attending a men's Bible study in a nearby town, had God speak to him out of Exodus 14. This passage tells when Moses was confronted with the Red Sea on one side and Egyptians on the other. The Lord was speaking to Bob confirming in him that he was to become the pastor of the church in the small community. Bob, argued with the Lord, "but, Lord, I could not come up with a sermon every week." Bob clearly heard God say, "Bob, you won't but I will." God was faithful to what He said and for the next 11 years enabled Bob to pastor and teach the people.

§

From April's journal Feb. 2020: "I heard the word 'unmitigated hope' during the night last night. 'This is not a word I typically use.' The definition of 'unmitigated' is absolute, complete or not lessened. (It was interesting that I heard this right before the Covid-19 Pandemic hit)."

§

Corey has a wonderful spiritual gift mix and with his compassion he has learned to listen to the Lord and then walk in obedience. It is not unusual for Corey to give every dime he has in his pocket to a needy person in obedience to the voice of the Lord. He just listens, sometimes it is one single word, like "compassion" or sometimes it is just an impression like, "they are the ones I want you to clothe, or feed, or put up in a hotel room..."

§

Marjorie writes, "God takes care of me in the funniest ways. We needed new pillows, but with the myriad of choices I had not gotten around to doing the research. We went to Missoula, Montana for my daughter's acting seminar. I saw advertised a farmer's market. I thought I should go to look at the jams, jellies and fresh vegetables that are usually available at these markets. When we got there, there was a whole tent selling nothing but pillows. I thought, 'I am supposed to buy pillows and here they are.'"

§

"I am famous for losing my keys and my checkbook. When losing them, I always ask the Holy Spirit their location and all of the time He very specifically tells me where they are. 'They are in your purse...They are in the car...They are on the counter.'"

§

During Lamar and Linda Taylor's time at LIFE Bible College, their passion to be missionaries had been fanned into flame. Lamar says, "In 1990, we were pastoring of a small church in western Colorado. That year, our divisional superintendent was taking a mission team to Sri Lanka and asked us to join the team. We spent 12 days in Sri Lanka, ministering in a pastors' conference and preaching and ministering in some of the outlying areas. Linda and I both saw the potential need for ministry in Sri Lanka and thought we could be used there. As we were flying out of Sir Lanka, Linda sensed the voice of the Lord saying, 'It's not the need that calls; it's Me.' Since then, we have spent time in South Korea and have been on mission trips to Guatemala and Chile, but we have not been back to Sri Lanka.

§

Gabe and Joelle were platonic roommates who fought constantly. Their common denominator was they went to the same church and both loved the Lord. Gabe and Joelle went on a mountain outing where Gabe planned to get off by himself and seek the Lord. On the drive back to town, Gabe said to Joelle, "I asked God who my mate was to be, and He told me it was you." Joelle responded, "We would kill each other in the first week. But I will pray about it, and if the Lord confirms I will follow His will." Joelle took the matter to prayer and heard the distinctive words, audible to her, "Yes you are supposed to marry Gabe." Joelle calls it the "wedding proposal from God." Today Gabe and Joelle are powerful together, as a married couple, in their ministry for the Lord

§

Monica was in the throes of divorce reeling, grieving, and hurting. One morning while blow drying her hair she distinctly heard the words, "pray for him." Monica said, "it was the last thing I wanted to do, but it was what God wanted me to do." This obedience was the first step to forgiveness!

§

Anna described the cloudy overcast day her husband and brother had gone to Laramie to a football game. Anna says, "I had planned to pick the apples from off of our apple tree...the task of picking all of the apples seemed daunting especially the apples in the top of the tree. I asked the Lord, 'Lord how will I be able to reach all of the apples, especially the ones in the top of the tree?' I heard nothing. Much to my surprise I went outside and every apple from the tree were all laying on the ground in a perfect line, not one apple was on top of another and none of the apples had evidence of bruising." Anna said, "that was the day when God picked my apples for me."

§

Suzanne said, "I was going to the grocery store and on the way, I passed the Grace Fellowship building. While passing the church I heard God say, 'I want you to go to church there.' At the time I did not know if it was really God speaking or if it was just me thinking. So, I told God that if that was Him speaking that my husband would say something about going to church in the next few days. Soon after on another trip to the grocery store, I came through the back door with the groceries, and my husband John came around the corner out of his office and said, 'We should start going to church, You pick which one and we will go this next weekend.' I knew right then God was telling us to go to Grace Fellowship."

§

After a painful divorce Tina was starting to doubt God's love for her. She had moved in with her mother and started working at a glass shop cutting glass and repairing window screens. One afternoon about 1:30 she went into the back room to pray. She asked God to not leave her or be too upset with her. A customer came in so the conversation with the Lord was cut short. That evening the phone rang and it was a person that Tina did not particularly care for, as they had previously had some conflicts on a board when they had served together. The lady on the other end of the phone said, "God spoke to me at 1:30 today and asked me to pray for you and call you. Again at 6 o'clock I felt God told me to call you."

She continued, "I thought that if it comes to my mind again, I will call." The caller confessed that she really did not want to call. (Tina thought under her breath I didn't want you to call either). God wanted the caller to give Tina a very specific message: "God wants you to know that He is watching over you and you should not be afraid. He is not going to abandon you and you are going to be alright." Tina thanked the lady for calling and after hanging up the phone, immediately heard the word, "I have heard your prayer." Tina later said, "If one of my friends had called, I would have been grateful to them, but God used someone I was not particularly fond of to let me know that He was serious."

§

Marlyce went to the local grocery store one late afternoon and on her way into the store noticed a young lady in the parking repacking her mountain climbing gear into her van. On the way out of the store, she noticed her again and had a brief and pleasant verbal exchange. When Marlyce was driving away the Holy Spirit strongly impressed on her heart to offer the young lady a shower and a bed for the night. Marlyce later said, "I had never done anything like that before." Kathy gladly accepted, and followed Marlyce home for a shower, a meal and a good night's sleep. It was a divine appointment as Kathy had recently been badly burned by some of her friendships and Marlyce was able to minister the love of Jesus to her. The two ladies have continued contact since that night.

§

Eva said: "After being in Colorado for 25 years one morning I woke up very impressed about a dream I had, and I shared that with my husband Daniel who is a man of God, I love and respect. In my dream I saw Daniel and I feeding people in a place that was dry and very hot. The dream stayed with me for months and months until we both came to the conclusion that it was God speaking to us. Later that year we came to El Paso Texas for a family reunion and as soon as we entered the city, I knew this was the hot and very dry city I saw in my dream. I almost cried and as soon as I could that afternoon I got on my knees and talked to God and told Him 'You know Lord how intolerant I am with heat.' I continued 'and this is such a huge place for me and Daniel; but if You are calling us here confirm it to us by giving me joy about it.' We both agreed to wait on the Lord for His perfect timing and two years later the Lord opened the door for us to relocate to El Paso. We have peace and are excited to see His plan developing, so with this and many other stories in our lives Daniel and I can say 'God still speaks, and we know His voice.'"

§

Marjorie said, "In the beginning of my walk with the Lord, while driving on an errand, I heard, as clear as a bell, 'Go see Lynn.' It was so clear I immediately did a U-turn in order to go visit with Lynn. Her son answered the door and was with her since she had received a difficult diagnosis. I asked him if she felt up to a visit. We visited for a couple of hours; Lynn passed away three days later. I am so glad I heard and listened to God's voice that day."

End Notes

Chapter One

Francis Frangipane, Spiritual Discernment and the Mind of Christ, (Arrow Publications, Inc. IA. 2013) 28.

Henry T Blackaby and Claude V King, Experiencing God, (LifeWay Press, TN 1990) 74.87.

Dallas Willard, Hearing God, (InterVarsity IL 2012) 287.

Chapter Three

F.B. Meyer, The Secret of Guidance, (Merchant Books 2018) 21-22. (Catherine of Siena was an Italian saint would lived in the 14th Century).

James W. Goll, Hearing God's Voice Today, (Chosen Books, MN 2016) 44.

Priscilla Shirer, Discerning the Voice of God, (Lifeway Press, TN 2017) 87.

Quoted by John Synder, Behold Your God, (Media Gratiae, MS 2013) 53.

Henri Nouwen, Spiritual Direction, (HarperOne, NY 2006) 93.

James W. Goll, Ibid. 73.

Ibid. 71.

Priscilla Shirer, Ibid. 86.

Kris Vallotton, Basic Training for the Prophetic Ministry- Study Guide, (Destiny, PA 2015) 54.

A J Sherrill, Quiet, (CreateSpace, SC, 2014) 9.

Mark Batterson, Whisper, (Multnomah 2017) 10.

Ibid. 11.

Dallas Willard, Hearing God, (InterVarsity press, IL 2012) 118.

Brother Lawrence, The Practice of the Presence of God, (Whittaker House, PA 1982) 475 of 710 Kindle Edition.

Henry T. Blackaby and Claude V. King, Experiencing God, (LifeWay Press, TN 1990) 88.

Chapter Four

Jack Deere, Surprised by the Voice of God (Zondervan, 1996) 312.

W.E. Vine, Vine's Expository Dictionary of Old and New Testament Words,(Thomas Nelson Publishers 1997)1.

Dictionary.com, (accessed July 2020).

Timothy Keller, Prodigal God, (Riverhead Books, 2008) 49.

Dallas Willard, Hearing God, (InterVarsity, 2012) 258.

Priscilla Shirer, Discerning the Voice of God, (LifeWay , 2017) 79.

A.W. Tozer https://www.goodreads.com/quotes/417895, (accessed 7/28/2020)

Chapter Five

Henry T. Blackaby and Claude V. King, Ibid. 65.

Dallas Willard, Hearing God, (InterVarsity press, IL 2012) 71.

Mark Batterson, Whisper (Multnomah, 2017) 102.

Chapter Six

Chris Tiegreen, The One Year Heaven on Earth Devotional: 365 Daily Invitations to Experience God's Kingdom Here and Now, (Tyndale, 2015) 26.

Charles Hummel (Goodreads.com/author/quotes/38456.Charles_E_Hummel) accessed 8/20.

F B Meyer, The Secret of Guidance, (Merchant Books, 1896 reprinted 2018) 27.

Priscilla Shirer, Discerning the Voice of God, (LifeWay 2017) 109.

Brother Yun and Paul Hattaway, Living Water, (Zondervan, 2008) Kindle Version 131-132.

Chapter Seven

www.healthline.com/health/pregnancy/when-can-a-fetus-hear#Will-my-baby-to-be-recognize-my-voice? (accessed 7/20).

Henry T. Blackaby and Claude V. King Experiencing God, (Lifeway 1990) 15.

Dallas Willard, Hearing God, (InterVarsity Press, 2012) 93.

http://www.latin-dictionary.net/ (accessed 8/2020).

Francis Frangipane, Spiritual Discernment and the Mind of Christ, (Arrow Publications 2013) 98.

Bill Johnson, Experience the Impossible, (Chosen Books 2014) 168.

Chapter Eight

Henri Nouwen, Spiritual Direction, (HarperOne 2006) 18.

Mark Batterson, Whisper, (Multnomah, 2017) 41.

Francis Frangipane, Spiritual Discernment and the Mind of Christ, (Arrow, 2013) 25.

A.W. Tozer, The Root of the Righteous, (Moody, 2015) 27-28.

Henri Nouwen, Ibid. 88.

Batterson, Ibid. 56-57.

Chapter Nine

Jennie Allen, Get Out of Your Head, (Waterbrook, 2020) 70.

Dallas Willard, Hearing God, (InterVarsity 2012) 94.

Mark Batterson, Whisper, (Multnomah, 2017) 2.

www.techopedia.com/definition/27898/gray-noise (accessed 7/20).

James and Patti Virkler, Communion With God Study Guide, (Destiny Image 1986, reprinted 1990) 43.

F B Meyer The Secret of Guidance, (Merchant Books, 1896 reprinted 2018) 7.

Chapter Ten

Dallas Willard, Hearing God, (InterVarsity 2012) 282.

Life Application Study Bible notes, (Tyndale House Publishers, IL. 2005) 1995.

Fire Bible Modern English Version, Study Bible, (Life Publishers 2015) 571.

Jack Deere, Surprised by the Voice of God, (Zondervan, 1996) 314.

Chapter Eleven

Bill Johnson, Experience the Impossible, (Chosen, 2014) 49.

Jack Deere, Surprised by the Voice of God, (Zondervan, 1996) 40.

Dallas Willard, Hearing God, (InterVarsity , 2012) 51.

A J Sherrill, Quiet, (CreateSpace 2014) 40.

Andrew Murray Draper's Book of Quotations, (Tyndale, 1992) 325.

Jack Deere, Ibid. 67.

Bill Johnson, Ibid. 226.

D.L. Moody, Drapers Book of Quotations, (Tyndale, 1992) 324.

Chapter Twelve

A J Sherrill, Quiet, (CreateSpace, 2014) 61.

Henri Nouwen, Spiritual Direction, (HarperOne, 2006) 97.

John 15:4 J.B. Phillips Translation, (The New Testament in Modern English by J.B Phillips copyright © 1960. 1972 J. B. Phillips, Administered by The Archbishops' Council of the Church of England. Used by Permission).

Chapter Thirteen

Francis Frangipane, Spiritual Discernment and the Mind of Christ, (Arrow Publications, 21013) 11.

Kris Vallotton, Basic Training for the Prophetic Ministry, (Destiny, 2015) 61.

Jack Deere, Surprised by the Voice of God, (Zondervan, 1996) 194.

Concluding Thoughts

Fellow Ships Music (SESAC) / So Essential Tunes (SESAC) / (admin at EssentialMusicPublishing.com). All rights reserved. Used by permission.

Works Cited

Allen, Jennie. *Get Out of Your Head* (Waterbrook, 2020).

Batterson, Mark. *Whisper* (Multnomah 2017).

Blackaby, Henry T and King, Claude. *Experiencing God* (LifeWay Press, TN 1990).

Deere, Jack. *Surprised by the Voice of God* (Zondervan, 1996).

Dictionary.com (accessed July 2020).

Fire Bible Modern English Version, Study Bible (Life Publishers 2015).

Frangipane, Francis. *Spiritual Discernment and the Mind of Christ* (Arrow Publications, Inc. IA. 2013).

Goll, James W. *Hearing God's Voice Today* (Chosen Books, MN 2016).

Healthline.com/health/pregnancy/when-can-a-fetus-hear#Will-my-baby-to-be-recognize-my-voice? accessed 7/20.

Hummel, Charles. (Goodreads.com/author/quotes/38456.Charles_E_Hummel) accessed 8/20.

J.B. Phillips Translation (The New Testament in Modern English by J.B Phillips copyright © 1960, 1972 J. B. Phillips, Administered by The Archbishops' Council of the Church of England. Used by Permission).

Johnson, Bill. *Experience the Impossible* (Chosen Books 2014).

Johnson, Jenn. Fellow Ships Music (SESAC) / So Essential Tunes (SESAC) / (admin at EssentialMusicPublishing.com). All rights reserved. Used by permission.

Keller, Timothy. *Prodigal God* (Riverhead Books, 2008).

Latin Dictionary. http://www.latin-dictionary.net/ (accessed 8/2020).

Lawrence, Brother. *The Practice of the Presence of God* (Whittaker House, PA 1982) 475 of 710 Kindle Edition.

Life Application Study Bible notes (Tyndale House Publishers, IL. 2005).

Meyer, F.B. *The Secret of Guidance* (Merchant Books 2018).

Moody, D.L. *Drapers Book of Quotations* (Tyndale, 1992).

Murray, Andrew. *Draper's Book of Quotations* (Tyndale, 1992).

Nouwen, Henri. *Spiritual Direction* (HarperOne, NY 2006).

Sherrill, A.J. *Quiet* (CreateSpace, SC, 2014).

Shirer, Priscilla. *Discerning the Voice of God* (Lifeway Press, TN 2017).

Synder, John., *Behold Your God* (Media Gratiae, MS 2013).

Techopedia. www.techopedia.com/definition/27898/gray-noise, (accessed 7/20).

Tiegreen, Chris. *The One Year Heaven on Earth Devotional: 365 Daily Invitations to Experience God's Kingdom Here and Now* (Tyndale, 2015).

Tozer A.W. https://www.goodreads.com/quotes/417895 (accessed 7/28/2020)

---, *The Root of the Righteous* (Moody 2015).

Vallotton, Kris. *Basic Training for the Prophetic Ministry-* Study Guide (Destiny, PA 2015).

Vine, W.E. *Vine's Expository Dictionary of Old and New Testament*

Words (Thomas Nelson Publishers 1997).

Virkler, James and Patti. *Communion With God* Study Guide (Destiny Image 1986, reprinted 1990) 43.

Willard, Dallas. *Hearing God* (InterVarsity IL 2012).

Yun, Brother and Hattaway, Paul. *Living Water* (Zondervan, 2008) Kindle Version.

About The Author

Paul A. Gilbert

Paul is the lead pastor of Grace Fellowship in Buffalo, Wyoming. Paul teaches and equips believers to walk in their spiritual giftings and activation of the eyes and ears of their heart to maximize spiritual effectiveness. Paul is also the author of Developing Your Kingdom Eyes!

You may contact Paul at Pastorpaulgracefellowship@gmail.com

Books By This Author

Developing Your Kingdom Eyes

We know most of what happened to our first parents when they ate of the forbidden fruit in the Garden of Eden, the entrance of sin and the loss of intimate fellowship with God. But what happened to the way they saw? Their seeing was drastically changed. Their spiritual sight, an amazing gift from God, was lost. What the first Adam lost in his failure, the second Adam, Jesus, regained in His victory. I want to invite you on a journey to see how what was lost can be regained. How you can develop this blessing of being able to see spiritually. How your eyes can be opened.

Made in the USA
Coppell, TX
27 June 2021